HF 5549. 𐬺 S0-BMY-228

Rae, Leslie.

Evaluating trainer
 effectiveness

DATE DUE

FEB 0 4 2000		
FEB 0 7 2019		

DEMCO 38-297

EVALUATING TRAINER EFFECTIVENESS

EVALUATING TRAINER EFFECTIVENESS

Leslie Rae

BUSINESS ONE IRWIN
Homewood, Illinois 60430

This publication is designed to provide accurate and
authoritative information in regard to the subject matter
covered. It is sold with the understanding that neither the
author nor the publisher is engaged in rendering legal, accounting,
or other professional service. If legal advice or other expert
assistance is required, the services of a competent
professional person should be sought.

*From a Declaration of Principles jointly adopted by a Committee
of the American Bar Association and a Committee of Publishers.*

Sponsoring editor: Cynthia A. Zigmund
Project editor: Rebecca Dodson
Production manager: Diane Palmer
Designer: Heidi J. Baughman
Art coordinator: Heather Burbridge
Compositor: BookMasters, Inc.
Typeface: 11/13 Times Roman
Printer: The Book Press, Inc.

Library of Congress Cataloging-in-Publication Data

Rae, Leslie.
    Evaluating trainer effectiveness / Leslie Rae.
        p.   cm.
    Includes index.
    ISBN 1-55623-881-9
    1. Employee training personnel—Rating of. 2 Employees—Training
of—Evaluation. I. Title.
HF5549.5.T7R244   1993
658.3'12404—dc20   92–37513

Printed in the United States of America
1 2 3 4 5 6 7 8 9 0 BP 9 8 7 6 5 4 3 2

Preface

If you're a training manager, how many times have you thought or even said to yourself: I think so-and-so (one of my trainers) is good, but

- How good?
- How good compared with others?
- How good should they be?
- How do I know?

Similarly, if you're a trainer, whether you work in a commercial or industrial organization, in a dedicated training organization, or as a training consultant, have you asked the same questions of yourself?

I suspect these questions have been asked many times in both situations, because the information is needed to ensure efficiency and effectiveness and for development. What's more, trainers as a "breed" tend to be more self-critical and questioning than many other professions or occupations.

Having thought these questions, what have you done about trying to obtain objective answers? On so many occasions the only action is to think: Yes. He/she is a good trainer. I don't know how or why I say that (others say so), (he/she seems to get results), (the trainees seem to like him/her), (etc.), I just know.

Fortunately these feelings can be correct, perhaps more often about somebody else than oneself, because we are consciously or subconsciously picking up various signals. These signals produce the "effective trainer" image in our minds—even though we are unable to say how we reached that conclusion.

It would be much more useful to explore these factors in a more objective and analytical way. In some cases, this approach is essential when people at a higher authority level say, "So you/he/she are/is a good trainer? Tell me how you know." The answer "I just know" is not acceptable. Perhaps you may feel the unacceptability of this response yourself without the demands of role boundary pressure. This book is intended to help trainers and others concerned with the quality of training to answer such questions as:

- What is an effective trainer?
- What are the skills of an effective trainer?
- Are we certain we are looking for the appropriate skills?
- What are the appropriate skills for my trainers/for me?
- What are the appropriate training skills for this industry/ organization?
- How do I assess these skills and achievements?
- Are there standards with which I can compare my assessments?
- Which skills need to be developed—how and why?
- How can I maintain a control of these skill levels?

These questions exercise (or should exercise) the minds of training directors, training managers, trainers, consultants, and line managers. I have for some time managed trainer workshops for the Institute of Training and Development on this subject at which these questions have been raised; introduced a complete trainer assessment system into a large organization because they wanted answers to these questions; had the questions posed to me by individuals; and asked them of myself!

We must not forget the other side of the equation—our clients are interested in the subject too. The managers who are providing trainees want to know how skilled the trainer is and this information will help them in deciding whether or where to send their people for training. Unless the manager has encountered the trainer previously, as a trainee or learner, on attending a training event, the questions in his mind may not be about the training itself but

- What is the trainer going to be like?
- Will I like him/her?
- Will I be able to relate to him/her?
- Will I be able to learn from him/her?

Even though "things" are necessary, people are more important than things.

The generic "he," "his," "him" are used throughout the book for the sake of brevity and to avoid the ridiculous situations created by the use of plurals. Consequently, for "he" also read "she."

Leslie Rae

Contents

Chapter One

The Role of the Trainer

For many years, training was not recognized as a separate entity. Newcomers to an occupation usually learned their trade on the job, and sitting with Mary or John was the most common form of introduction to work. At worst, they were told that "x" was the best "y" in the organization and if they watched him, they would quickly learn the job. In most cases, "x" was much more interested in getting on with the job, and thus earning money, than teaching someone else to do it. The "learner" sat beside Mary or John and watched, trying to make sense out of what was being done. Soon the manager or supervisor would declare that because the learner had seen what had to be done, he should now be able to do it. And so the newcomer was given his own workstation and left to do the job.

At the other end of the spectrum, we find a skilled and experienced worker, equipped by the organization with the skills of work force training. This approach is exemplified in the well-known, although now defunct, TWI (Training Within Industry). It concentrated on the better aspects of the Mary/John method of training by encouraging organizations to train their "on-the-job trainers" in the skills of this method. Selected workers who had the job skills and the potential to learn to be trainers were taught job analysis, job instruction design and techniques, and so on. "Tell, show, do" became part of the training language as a result of this type of training. On-the-job trainers were given time to prepare for their training sessions and produce job training manuals or instruction sheets. Eventually these became the job training manuals now used by many industries. The newcomer was introduced to Mary/John, who might describe the task and its functions and show the learner the task in operation, at the same time describing what was happening and why. The learner, under the observation of the trainer, would then attempt the task or parts of it, until it was obvious he was capable of performing it to the required standard. The learner might then progress to the actual work, under strict supervision, and ideally in the early stages Mary/John would monitor the results of the training.

THE DEVELOPMENT OF TRAINING

The change from "sit down and learn" to the supported training by an on-the-job trainer required not only an improvement in training methods, but also a change in attitude to training. While a newcomer was being trained in this more effective manner, the production that would have otherwise come from Mary/John was lost. The employer was persuaded to accept this loss because it was now obvious the newcomer would learn more quickly and effectively and become an efficient producer much more speedily. Because the learner was more efficient when starting production, less waste would result. These changes produced a decrease in costs, over a slightly longer term, despite the apparent short-term increase in cost.

The group approach in education had long been appreciated, but when the educational processes were transferred to training they continued as the didactic, sit and listen and learn approach. Courses consisted of either a series of lectures given by the trainers or a similar series presented by guest speakers or visiting "experts," who were experts in the subject, but not necessarily in the techniques of presentation. It was during this era that methods, albeit subjective and restricted, of assessing a trainer's skill were developed. As the trainer was only delivering lectures, or similar forms of input, these assessments were concerned with presentational skills.

This approach to training continued for many years, although one or two more enlightened trainers or organizations questioned its value and moved into more varied forms of training.

Research by educational and industrial psychologists showed that the lecture form of training, where the learners sat passively and were expected to accept information and be able to translate this into skills, was often not the most effective method.

LEARNING BY DOING

The training era of experiential learning, or learning by doing, was dawning and all indications were that if you did something instead of listening to people talk, you would return to work with some skill.

The disillusioned trainers grasped this concept willingly, because many of them were as bored as their trainees with the interminable lectures. Training courses ceased to follow the traditional lecture form and became periods of intense activity, exercise, and game playing. In many cases, this swing from the lecture to the game was extreme, and trainers soon realized experiential training was not the panacea it had appeared to be.

Most employers at this stage paid little attention to training, and many were suspicious of its value. They had seen their staff who had attended the lecture type of training return bored and uninterested and rarely put into practice anything they had learned. Now they saw them returning full of the games they had played and saying how enjoyable the experience had been, but little learning seemed to have occurred.

With a greater understanding of how people learn effectively came the realization that neither the lecture, nor the activity approach, nor many of the other alternatives were ineffective. People are different in the ways they learn, and because the trainee population is heterogeneous, the most effective form of training likely to suit the majority of this mixed population would be a training approach (not necessarily a course) with a varied content. This content would obviously not suit all the learners, all the time, but most would benefit greatly, and some would at least learn something valuable.

VARIED FORMS OF LEARNING

In addition to changes in the training approach, training departments looked at the increasing number of learning aids available—films, videos, interactive videos, training packages, self-learning packages, computer-based and computer-assisted learning, and so on. With these new methods, learning through training should now be universal and more effective. Most subjective indications suggest this is so; subjective because there is little real evidence about the limitations of the traditional methods and only limited objective evidence of the success of current approaches. Improvements do seem to be occurring, however. As a result, individuals and organizations are starting to take training and development more seriously.

Now, a trainer is required to be a person of high flexibility, knowledge, and skills, able to introduce the most effective elements required by the situation.

In the 1960s, creativity became a buzzword for training efforts within corporate America. Consultants fostered radical approaches to problems affecting productivity. During the 70s and 80s, this approach produced many quality circle type efforts. With the economic downturn, these worker-involved, facilitator-led training and problem-solving efforts cooled. The past two years have seen a dramatic rebirth in this country of the creativity approach as the corporate world decided creativity might not be a talent, but rather a learned skill.

TRAINING AND DEVELOPMENT

Two words have assumed much more importance in recent years—*learning* and *development*. The move from *training* to *learning* has accompanied the many changes in training methods. One of the principal changes has involved the shift in control of the learning event. With the trainer in the driver's seat, the trainees had no option other than accept the directives of the trainer. The more participative mode of training means the learners gain some control of the learning process, and in certain cases some of the content. Some feared this might lessen the amount of material learned; but in most cases, the learners demanded a more extensive range and depth of material.

For many, the ultimate type of learning is through the workshop, rather than the training course. In the workshop, the learners may decide to a large extent the content and extent of the workshop, the time necessary to process this learning, the method of the learning and its review and monitoring. The trainer's role changes radically; he becomes a resource for the learners, to be called on to provide information, experiences, skill assistance, resources, support, and so on. As this demands the wider range of skills referred to earlier, the trainer ceases to be the traditional, "presentational" type of trainer, which places more demands on him than preparing his sessions within the limits of his knowledge and skills. The trainer retains control of the process in the truest sense.

A change is required not only in the methods of the trainer, or facilitator, but also in his attitude. In giving up the reins, he may also have to accept that he is not the universal expert—and does not need to be.

Development is a word used widely and often loosely, sometimes as a synonym for *training*. It has a wider meaning than training, which tends to be usually a singular learning activity, such as a training course, workshop, or learning package. Development can be considered as an overall approach to an individual's or group's improvement and enhancement. It can involve a series of training events of various types, which preferably lead to a total learning experience that leaves the learner stronger.

The advent of *development* demonstrates yet another change in the attitudes applied to training. Originally, training, like education, was looked on as a series of isolated events that were identified and developed in isolation and produced a sum of knowledge and skills. In the development approach, each event is linked and relevant to every other event and to the total requirements of the learner and the organization.

The development aspect of training, with discussion on course content, demonstrates this desirable change in attitude and process. The need for discussion suggests the trainer is not only much more involved in the training/learning with the learner, but also with another person with a responsibility in the process—the learner's supervisor.

THE LEARNING TRINITY

The line supervisor has always been responsible for the training and, particularly, the development of the staff. Traditionally, supervisors have regarded training as the province of the trainer because training was not "work," and, after all, the trainers were the experts in training. In many cases, training course participants were there because they had been told to go and be trained, whether or not they wanted or needed it. The emphasis on development, rather than just training, requires a considered approach and more involvement by line management. After all, the learners do not work for the trainers. They must train and develop to ensure that the job is carried out in the most effective way, which would benefit their immediate supervisor. In many cases, when a training/learning need arose at work, it was simple to send the person to a training course. This absolved the line supervisors from doing anything themselves and allowed them to transfer the problem, albeit temporarily, to the trainer.

But as training moves to a wider developmental structure, the need arises for an effective "training trinity." This trinity consists of the line supervisor, the trainer, and the learner. The roles within the training trinity are generally well defined, although there must be a certain amount of overlap.

Line Management

Although the skills of the trainer are essential, the active involvement of the line supervisor is critical. The trainees are direct employees of the line supervisor and need his practical support:

- To determine individual, as opposed to corporate need.
- To encourage and actively support the satisfaction of needs, whether these have been identified by the individual or by the line supervisor.
- To ensure the needs are met in the most appropriate manner and at the relevant time.
- To support actively the trainees on their return from or completion of the learning event.
- To ensure development is a continuing process rather than an isolated event.

Managers must be aware of the learning opportunities available and work closely with the trainer.

Once it has been decided that training is required, with or without the early involvement of the trainer, the line supervisor can discuss with the trainer how needs can be met and agree with the trainer on the most appropriate approach.

Before the training, the line supervisor must conduct a precourse briefing session with the learner to discuss the final details and agree about training objectives for the individual and for the organization, both local and corporate. At this stage, the need for the training will be confirmed and the most relevant method agreed on.

Agreement is needed about a date for the line supervisor and trainee to meet soon after the end of the training. Without such a meeting, the learner might believe the supervisor has little or no interest in what is happening, that his absence from work is almost irrelevant, and there will be a similar lack of interest on his return.

In the post-course debriefing meeting, the line supervisor and trainee will discuss what occurred during the training, what learning was achieved, what action plans were made, and arrange future support and action. The trainer can become involved for at least part of the discussion, particularly when the line supervisor may not be able to cope with the situation or the problems may be too large for a nonexpert to satisfy. The trainer should be there solely in a support role. The discussion should be between the manager and the trainee, and the trainer must resist either the temptation or the implied invitation to take over.

In the complex corporate structures, the need for support goes to even higher levels. The trainee and his supervisor must know the training effort is supported up through the organization; if not, a level of acceptance and desire on the part of the trainee and supervisor is lost and with it the likely long-term value of the training to the corporation. One consistent problem of training efforts is the lack of understanding of that training at higher levels and a real or perceived devaluing of the training, which filters back to the trainee and supervisor.

The Trainer

Many of the trainer's activities within the trinity relationship are traditional ones. He must become actively involved early in the discussion of training needs, who should be trained, when, in which specific areas, where, and so on. In the past, trainers commonly were told of these requirments and had to react accordingly.

In an ideal relationship, both the line supervisor and the trainer should work jointly to investigate the job and people requirements leading to training needs identification. The trainer should also involve the line supervisors in developing course objectives and constructing the training program—the line supervisor brings the expertise of job knowledge; the trainer supplies the training and training program expertise.

The line supervisor can be brought into an active role in the training program itself by being introduced into the program as the expert on matters of the line; discussing real-life management problems; raising such questions as what the line supervisor expects of his staff; and so on. Including line supervisors can often add credibility to a training program. At a minimum, it enhances the trainees' impression of the thoroughness of the training by providing a context to the training from real-life situations with which the trainee identifies.

In many organizations, the traditional role of the trainer stops when the training has been completed. But this partnership needs a more continuing role. Although the debriefing of the trainee must remain the responsibility of the line supervisor, part of the debriefing—advice on implementation, further or alternative learning, and so on—can be enhanced by the trainer's involvement. The trainer may become actively involved in the continued learning at work, although this will depend on his availability. Care must be taken that the managerial responsibilities are not simply passed to the trainer to ease the manager's work or because the supervisor simply does not wish to perform these duties.

Another potentially contentious issue in the discussion of roles is evaluation, the long-term assessment in cost-benefit terms of the training. It can be argued that this is a continuation of the training event and the validation of that event and thus the responsibility of the trainer to follow through. The counterargument is that improvement in cost-effectiveness occurs within the line operation, and consequently the line supervisor should be responsible for the evaluation.

There can be no doubt that the supervisor is in the most appropriate position to assess by observation and the analysis of production results the long-term success of the training and any improvements that may be the result of the training.

The most effective evaluation involves a cooperative approach between the trainer and the supervisor. A typical evaluation exercise could be follow-up questionnaires sent by the trainer to both the trainees and their supervisors, followed by clarification and diagnostic interviews that will confirm both views. The supervisor is in a position to observe the trainee more closely. If a full practice of validation and evaluation has been followed, control groups will have been included in the evaluation. The trainer is in a better position to maintain contact with these groups, while having constant contact with their supervisors. By working together, the trainer provides the expertise in training follow-up and the supervisor the expertise in operational improvement assessment.

The Trainee or Learner

Last, but far from least, is the trainee, without whom the whole exercise would have no value. In the past, little notice has been taken of the wishes and needs of the learner, but if they are ignored and what is provided does not meet with their wishes, little learning will result and the training will have been a waste of time.

When the concept of the training is being formulated, the potential trainees are involved in activities related to identifying the needs of the task and the level of competence of those performing the tasks or planned to perform the tasks—the determination of training needs. The ideal would be for the trainee to be directly involved in the planning of the training itself.

The extent to which the emphasis of training/learning ownership should be passed to the learner is an important element in the changing role of training. Time is now often allocated at the start of the training event for the necessary planning. In similar ways, the trainees can be involved in the validation of the event and the evaluation of the development program. Traditionally, the pre-training event tests, the interim validation measures, the end-of-course validations, and the long-term evaluation approaches were all constructed by the trainer and supervisor. These measures were then imposed on the trainee without question. More realistic and effective responses are likely if the trainees are given a more prominent role in the decisions about these validation measures. For example, the trainees could be asked to produce the end-of-course questionnaire or method they would find most acceptable and useful.

THE TRAINING QUINTET

Important as the three role-holders may be, two other elements must be considered if the training is to be completely effective. The training manager is of considerable importance, and without the organization, no training would be necessary. These two roles, added to the training trinity, produce the training quintet.

Organization

The organization, usually senior management, recognizes the need for training and sets guidelines for the training function, as statements of the developing needs of the organization. Developments in the medium and long term will suggest training needs.

The traditional approach, still all too common, has been to let the training section know when (and not until) the need arises. A more useful approach, particularly if the training quintet is to be of value, is to make it organizational policy to bring training and development into the earliest stages of discussion about future developments. In many cases, this requires a change of attitude toward training and development by senior management, who in the past have not always taken training and development too seriously.

Given ample warning of pending changes, the training section can ensure that any necessary action is planned in good time, thus allowing it to be planned more effectively. This has never been more evident than in the recent economic downturn in the United States. Companies, such as Ford Motor Co., turned inwardly in a combined effort with training, supervisors, workers, and upper management to address problems critical to continued operation of the corporation, and those solutions directly affected the corporate bottom line.

The training function has often been too distant from senior management to have this effect. If the training role is to develop into a positive force in the organization, the training department must be recognized and accepted by senior management as a force that can help the organization achieve its objectives. Much depends on the hierarchical status of the trainer, and it is in this area that the training manager, the fifth member of the quintet, is able to make a strong contribution.

The Training Manager

The training manager completes the quintet, although in some cases the trainer or training office and the training manager are the same person. In many ways, it is preferable if they have been trainers themselves—this is an extension of the classical argument about the need for a manager to be a subject expert. Specialist managers such as training managers need to have a very good working knowledge of training and development. Often their role includes not only management of the training function but also specific training duties, perhaps with more senior managers. They need to have a working knowledge of a wide range of training and learning methods, techniques and approaches, to aid them in assessing the trainers for whom they are responsible.

A number of different types of training manager exist, each with his own particular profile. At one extreme is the training manager who has no training staff, and, in addition to managing the training function itself—planning, designing, negotiating, budgeting, and so on—is also involved in direct training within the organization. These managers are not rare and often rely on external assistance to help them fulfill all the training demands. Usually they are found in small companies or small independent units of larger organizations. Their tasks can become very difficult to juggle—when they should be considering development of the training function, and in particular its cost, they are more likely to be called away to perform a training task.

At the other extreme is the training manager who has almost exclusively a management role. He has a training team of several trainers and may be responsible for a learning resource center and also for negotiation and control of a training budget. Most of the work of this manager is in managing; but because of the specialism, there is no excuse for not having an extensive knowledge of training.

Within the training quintet, the training manager has a very important and specific role. He will

- Develop training principles and programs with other members of the quintet.
- Support, in a managerial role, the trainer, ensuring that sufficient resources of whatever nature will be available.
- Participate in investigatory and research projects that will extend the range of learning facilities available.
- Negotiate during the early stages of a difficult liaison with line management to ensure the quintet develops into a viable working unit.

Most important, the training manager is often the link between supervisor and trainer, representing the training viewpoint and, more particularly, the conceptual and functional needs of training and development with the top decision-making levels of the organization. Many are not in positions to wield a reasonable power, but the training manager must take a proactive approach to ensure that the value of training is recognized and given the responsible position it deserves. On rare occasions, the training manager is invited to the first meetings of a working group, at whatever level in the organization, when new corporate projects are initiated. This early involvement ensures that potential training needs and activities are considered at this early stage.

The training manager is the linchpin, having interest in all aspects of training and development and also coordinating the interests and requirements of the other members of the quintet.

Developing a training quintet in an organization will enhance not only the value of the training department, but also the training itself. Senior management will look on training as part of the strategic partnership, or at least a tactical arm of that strategic force. Line management, traditionally suspicious of trainers, will, because they become so involved themselves, use training as a real part of their job and develop new working relationships. The learners will benefit and will cease to be pawns in the training versus "real world of work" chessboard. The trainers and the training manager will benefit because they will realize their value is being recognized and they have a place within the organization rather than being "that bunch in the training department."

THE ASSESSMENT FUNCTION IN TRAINING

For these benefits to become a reality, the training manager must ensure the training is performed to the best of the abilities of the trainers, the learners actually acquire some learning, and, with the support of the supervisor, the learning is applied in the workplace. These activities do not happen unaided; the purpose of this book is to suggest the ways and means this may be achieved.

Part of the role of the training manager must be to maintain training standards at a high level (however these might be defined). A program of assessing both the training and the trainers needs to be initiated, enhanced, or maintained, depending on current circumstances. My experience suggests that training managers assess their trainers as and when they can and to the best of their abilities. This usually means that from time to time, often at long intervals, the training manager sits in on a session of one of his trainers, leaves without giving realistic feedback other than "uhh, that was OK, wasn't it?" and that is that. Such "assessment" is not only unhelpful, but it can also be highly dangerous.

The training manager must be in frequent contact with the trainers and also the work of the trainers to (1) maintain high standards, (2) provide realistic feedback of performance to the trainers, and (3) support the annual appraisal system. The first and second reasons suggest a strict control and monitoring of defined standards. How this is performed is the effective part of the action. It must not be, or be seen to be, inspectorial, and the model suggested later in this book should soften this effect, although no degree of softening can take away the fact that an assessment of skill, efficiency, and effectiveness is occurring.

The training manager or other manager responsible for the training function must be the prime assessor in this activity, but my model suggests (1) this is done with agreement, and (2) parallel assessments are performed by the trainers themselves, by their peer or co-trainers, by the trainees directly, and, in a more indirect way, by the training itself. Even if "policing" is identified, much of this will be self-inflicted rather than externally imposed.

LINK WITH APPRAISALS

Where no trainer assessment system exists, the training manager and the remainder of the organization have no real measure of the skill of the training organization and, consequently, are more likely to either assume the worst or accept any negative feedback they receive from other sources. The trainers can become frustrated by lack of feedback about their performance, and interrelationships can become strained as suspicions arise.

An effective feedback system, however, can enhance not only the immediate feedback action, but also an annual appraisal system. These annual reviews can evolve in three ways: (1) they can be so cursory as to be meaningless; (2) they can evolve into discussions of future training efforts that trainers should undertake rather than any real feedback on training content or technique; or (3) in the worst case, they can devolve to a simple discussion of learner responses that were completed immediately following the training session.

Many appraisal systems rely on the annual formal report and performance review interview. This process can suddenly create ill feelings between the two people involved as previously unexpressed criticisms are raised. The appraiser has obviously saved up all the bullets for this interview, perhaps under the impression that this was the occasion when they should be fired. "Appraisals" of this nature can be traumatic and generate conflict, thus harming working relationships—"Why didn't he say that when it happened instead of waiting until now!"

Planned and continuous feedback ensures that there is at least the opportunity to make any comments—bad or good—nearer when the incidents occur. Immediate feedback also allows early rectification of any faults by the trainer, rather than a repair operation following the trauma of the "appraisal interview." Although the approach suggested by Blanchard in *The One Minute Manager* may be on the sparse side, the basic approach of praise them or kick them at the time is very relevant.

There are constraints. The more time the training manager allocates to trainer assessment, the less time there is for other essential activities.

There are communication tasks to be performed, administration to be kept efficient, negotiations with senior and line management to take place, reports to write, budgets to argue and maintain. The training manager's trainers are his most important resource—without them there is little reason to maintain a training department. But too often they are ignored for these administration reasons and sometimes because "I don't need to watch 'x' working; I know he's good and he doesn't need me to tell him."

Often trainers may not know whether they are good or not, or how good they are as measured against the standards, and they do need to be told by their boss. Technical and professional managers tend to be even less effective at giving feedback:

> After all, my people (trainers) are technically trained/professionals so they do not need to be kept informed about how they are doing.

Would that were so! In my experience, professional trainers tend to be less sure of themselves than others and need reassurances. Structured yet friendly, formal yet natural feedback, may be given without an excessive use of precious time.

Chapter Two

Trainer Requirements

The previous chapter reviewed the role of the trainer and his relationship with others in general terms. But what is the basic role of the trainer? What is a trainer? What are they expected to do? Are they all the same? These are some of the many questions that must be answered before you can assess how well you or they are performing.

TRAINING FUNCTIONS

The word *trainer* carries a wide range of meanings, stemming initially from the function the trainer performs.

The Workplace Instructor

On-the-job instructors should be skilled, experienced, and efficient operatives in the area of their normal employment. They must also possess:

- An interest and commitment to the development of other people (for the benefit of the organization as well as the individuals) to the extent that they will want to act as a trainer.
- An interest in helping other people to become proficient in a function of which they themselves may be proud:
- An innate ability or potential to learn to train, or a proven ability as a trainer.

Not all these interests or skills are evident without experience and practice, and many people who have a strong desire to train, and firmly believe they can, are found wanting when it comes to the actual practice. Many examples of this can be seen, none more evident than the parent who decides or agrees to teach his child to drive a car! The will is certainly there, and the driving experience and skill may also exist, and his training skills may have been proven in other areas, but because of the emotional factors involved, the normal skills of training do not seem to emerge and the training is a failure.

Emotions do not often interfere with straightforward face-to-face training in the workplace, although other factors have a similar effect. Often the "Mary/John" is given casually the job of training someone. Either the trainer, the learner, or the boss quickly discovers Mary/John is not a born trainer, or an innate ability emerges and a potential trainer is born. The farsighted employer will recognize this potential and will make formal training facilities available for "Mary/John" to learn how to be a fully efficient and effective trainer or instructor.

The Instructor

Mechanical, technical, and procedural tasks require a straightforward approach in which the emphasis is usually on the teacher-taught environment. Although both the teachers and the learners may want to approach the learning event in a different, more "enlightened" way, the training task demands that the subject is taught—at least in the earlier stages. Instructors in this environment must be highly self-disciplined and very knowledgeable about the subject, at least to the teaching level required and preferably beyond. They must have an up-to-date manual of instruction or procedural base from which to instruct; even a little variation from this approach is often impossible. In many cases, at least in the acquisition of knowledge, the instructor can be replaced by an artificial instructor in the form of a computer, video, audio cassette, or manual. But, a live instructor may be preferable, even if only to support the open learning approach. When it comes to applying the knowledge, the services of an instructor are necessary in most cases.

Particular types of trainers make good instructors. The worse type of trainer for this role is the one who insists on always saying, "Why do we do it like this?" "I would like to try something. It may not work, but it will be a variation," and so on. However, this attitude must be applied initially, or at some stage, to the instruction to ensure that challenges to the system have not been rejected because of apathy, hidebound tradition, instructor preferences, and corporate politics. If the approved method is really known to be the most appropriate, questioning or the questioner has a high nuisance value.

Although group instruction has existed for a long time, its use became widespread during World War II when many unskilled men and women had to be taught quickly the basic elements of jobs needed for the war effort. The training for these tasks was often broken into smaller parts that could be learned in sequence. The formal instructional methods known as TWI (Training Within Industry) also developed during this era. Because so many people had trained in this way, group instruction methods developed.

The mechanistic approach to training need not be without its lighter side to break the formality. On one occasion, an expert instructor was due to give an introductory session on the safe handling of explosives. He was only a few minutes into his session when a small but distinct explosion came from the back of the room. Pandemonium ensued among the learners for a while, but when the instructor was able to quiet them down he was able to tell them it had been a planned explosion with x pounds of explosives. He then invited them, many of whom had never experienced an explosion previously, to imagine the explosion with x^n pounds of explosives, the more usual charge. Learners gained more from this experience than from a film.

In another incident, a colleague of mine was required to tutor a training session on the social security regulations relating to Share Fishermen, a complicated, dull subject about statistics. This trainer was a very ebullient person and, after two extremely boring sessions, both for him and the learners, he decided to try something to lighten at least part of the session. Thirty seconds after the session was due to start he burst open the door and strode in wearing wellingtons, oilskins, and so'wester and carrying a fishing rod from which dangled half a plastic fish. A colleague threw half a bucket of water at him from outside in the corridor. Standing there in that outlandish garb, dripping with water and with the ridiculous fish dangling in front of him, he announced, "I've come to talk to you about Share Fishermen!" The group exploded with laughter. While he went on to conduct the session very much as before, the atmosphere was quite different and the learning vastly improved.

The Trainer/Tutor

The trainer/tutor is probably the largest category and will almost certainly remain so. Trainer/tutors are required to have wide knowledge of techniques, approaches, and methods. The principal activity is the presentation of training sessions, with or without the use of visual aids, linking the lecture with discussion or other activities. The trainer/tutor also leads discussion; sets, controls and debriefs role-plays, activities, and case studies; shows films and videos and links these with associated activities; controls and supports training packages, computer programs, and other supported learning systems; and so on. Often, the trainer designs the learning events and stays in control of most of the situation. He is the foundation of the large training department that relies on formal, structured training to satisfy the large-scale demands of the corporate population.

The Facilitator

As we saw in the previous chapter, training is increasingly moving away from the formal training course to events that are initially trainer-designed and led but quickly develop into workshops in which the learners are given more control of the event. In such cases, the trainer needs to have all the knowledge and skills of the trainer/tutor, but may need to be even more knowledgeable in view of the unforeseen demands the learners might make. So the available tool kit must be bulging with a wide range of roles, cases, activities, subject scenarios, and minisessions.

Above all, the facilitator must be able to stand back and present himself not as the expert, but rather as a resource, albeit a very skilled one, for the free use of the learners. He must be able to intervene or stay remote at the appropriate moments; to lead (with all the different meanings to the word); to offer relevant activities and then let the learners progress or regress, allowing them to dig themselves out of the holes they dug.

As organizations change their approaches to training and development from traditionally run courses to more human resource-related approaches, existing trainers need to develop into this wider role of facilitator. Many can make this transition, but some will be unable to let go of the reins. There is obviously a place for these in certain types of training and organizations.

Some corporations have shied away from using teachers as trainers. This directly relates to the ability to make the transition from the highly structured learning environment of academe to the fluidity of the facilitator role. As one human resource director said, "Teachers are often used to teaching people who *must* be there, while facilitators teach people who *want* to be there."

The Consultant/Adviser

Until recently, the corporate demand for educated consultancy and advice was satisfied almost exclusively by external agencies, composed of private consultants with a wide range of experience in industries and companies. The internal trainers, although experts in their own fields, did not always have the knowledge and skills necessary to offer wide-ranging advice. But many organizations, particularly the larger ones, have increasingly demanded their own internal consultants. They have found it beneficial to give internal agents, who are knowledgeable about the organization, its politics, its culture, its procedures, and its needs, the resources and time to expand their knowledge. The disadvantage of this is the danger that an internal consultant might be too inward looking.

Internal consultants, if they have corporate credibility, can tackle wider company needs through extensive, but inexpensive training needs analyses; become involved in more individual tutorials or advice with senior management; search for, and advise on, wider developmental opportunities, including those in the educational field; become the repository of an extensive library of information and views about training and development methods, centers of excellence that can be recommended; advise on appropriate avenues of learning; and so on.

It may be inappropriate to introduce hierarchies among trainers, but this happens. Some try to equate the status or skill level of operative, supervisor, and management training with "trainer levels." I believe this is unhelpful because all forms of training require different, not necessarily better, skills for the various groups. There does seem to be some advantage, however, in considering the skill hierarchy of the instructor and the trainer (if these two are differentiated because of training needs rather than skill or attitude), then the facilitator, and the consultant/adviser. The three types need to acquire skill, knowledge, techniques, and attitudes to progress from one position to the other. There will always be exceptions as to who can enter one or the other level without experiencing the skills of the preceding one, but successful practitioners of this nature are rare.

The Trainer of Trainers

This specialist group of trainers is found in organizations with relatively large training departments or in specialist training organizations such as BACIE (British Association for Commercial and Industrial Education), the Industrial Society, the Institute of Training and Development, the

American Society for Training and Development, and other more commercially based trainer training companies.

The basic problem is similar to that discussed earlier concerning the skills needed by managers; to what extent does the trainer of trainers need to have served an apprenticeship as a trainer before being allowed to enhance the skills of trainers? Does the trainer of trainers need to have been highly skilled and effective as a trainer? Or does one have to accept the derogatory suggestion, often quoted, "If you can't do it, teach it!"

The recruit to trainer training should be one of the most effective, skilled, and experienced trainers possible. Only trainers with this skill level have the credibility and the experience on which to draw to make their training widely applicable.

Otherwise, the role of the trainer of trainers is similar to that of the general trainer or facilitator, but with the ability to relate closely to the role of the learners and vice versa. Deliberately or not, desirable or not, they are presenting themselves as role models before the embryonic trainers. If they are seen to be performing in a particular way, some of the learners will copy this practice. For this reason, the training team must be carefully selected. In the training team I managed, I had the extrovert, boisterous, activist type of trainer; the serious, logical, well-prepared, fairly staid but absolutely reliable trainer; and the highly skilled, articulate, and "clever" trainer with strong facilitator tendencies. These three complemented each other, but also offered three of the possible role models for the learners to see in action.

The Training Designer

In recent years, the role of the training designer has developed and become a force that is strongly allied to classical training. Training events are ceasing to be isolated and are becoming complete packages. The training designer identifies and analyzes the needs of the learners and trainers and designs a total package. This might consist of a set of instructional briefs or a manual, with all the necessary master OHP slides, a video and accompanying trainers' and learners' handbooks, perhaps an audio cassette, all the required handouts either in collated sheet form or as a comprehensive booklet, and a trainer's guide to the whole package. The package is then tested and produced and made available as an off-the-shelf pack for trainers.

Not all the training in different organizations or different parts of one organization require the same approach, however. In such cases, the specific package can be too directive on content and methods. On the positive side, if the operating trainer is inexperienced, the structure eases his entry into training. The more experienced trainer is able to manipulate much of the provided material to suit his requirements. If time is limited and the trainer is not able to sit down and design his own training—and this can take a substantial amount of time—all or much of his material is presented in the package, which also provides the methods of presentation.

The role of the nontraining trainer can be compared with that of the consultant/manager of an internal resource center. Such a facility is more than just a library, although it contains books addressing supervisory, management, and professional/technical knowledge and skills. It also contains the widest possible range of files, videos, interactive videos, audio packages, computer programs, training packages, games, activities, role-plays, and so on. The linked consultant, who may also be the manager of the resource center, can guide the user of the center to the most appropriate resource in this valuable collection. Resource centers also need to provide any hardware necessary to use the resources, such as computers, audio equipment, and video playing equipment. But because most centers have restricted budgets, they place a greater emphasis on the skill and knowledge of the consultant/manager, who should be aware of where other available resources are located, a mammoth task.

Many organizations in the United States maintain valuable resource material for trainers. Organizations such as the American Society for Training and Development (ASTD) and the Association of Training & Employment Professionals (ATEP) maintain material expressly on training, and industry organizations can supply resources for virtually any field imaginable. For instance, accountants can draw on resources from the AICPA, and child welfare agencies can draw on the resources of the Child Welfare League of America. Every major industry has an organization and in many cases several that serve as repositories of material valuable to training within that industry. A number of industries have state, regional, national, and international associations to draw on for training materials.

Using these organizations as resources offers true value to the training department within a corporation. Membership in these organizations can often make available prepackaged training materials.

The government is also a source of training material. Large amounts of training material are on deposit with a number of federal agencies, especially within the Department of Labor.

The largest problem is not quantity of information, but quality of advice. If, for example, a learner asks for information on time management training, it is relatively simple to provide a list of books, videos, audiocassettes, computer interactive videos, and training courses available, a substantial amount of material. The next question would be "Which is best?" or "Which course should I follow?" To answer this question, the resource consultant needs to know the effectiveness of each of the resources available plus the learner's preferred or possible learning style. This is a nearly impossible task, which means the resource capability, however extensive, can never provide total advice.

No doubt there are other trainer roles of this nature, and many trainers fill multiple roles, either consecutively or concurrently. In assessing trainer effectiveness, it is necessary to identify, from the training manager's point of view, which type of trainer you require and, from the trainer's point of view, which type you need to be and/or want to be. There is little value in a trainer objecting to criticism or self-criticism of his skill as an instructor if all his energies are being directed at being a facilitator (and the organization wants an instructor). As a first step in the assessment of trainer effectiveness, the overall role or roles that need to be fulfilled must be defined. If you are the training manager, ensure that this role is the one you want and are assessing.

The very skilled trainer is able to cover all the roles as the need arises, although some are so different it is not just a question of skill, but rather one of attitude. A training manager, who is also a direct trainer and offers a number of facilitator events, told me recently he was incapable of taking on the role of instructor in its most restrictive sense. When he had to lead a very specific procedural session in which he was required as the oracle, saying, "This is what you do," he found that within a short time he would move into his facilitator role and say, "This is what you ought to do. How do you feel about that?" His move from the required highly directive, instructive role to a more natural reflective, flexible one was inappropriate in these circumstances.

The Training Manager

Although the effective trainer continually engages himself in self-assessment, much of this assessment is performed by the training manager. What is a training manager? A training manager is in charge of the training function, but the role is not that straightforward. It has been mentioned earlier that a training manager can take on a variety of forms: a training manager with no staff or a training and administrative staff all rolled into one; a training manager with no staff who contracts out all the training to external providers and consequently is almost completely an administrative manager; a training manager with no personal training involvement but with a team of trainers and administrators, a manager in all senses of the word.

The culture and needs of the organization determine the roles for the training manager, much as he determines those of the training staff. As a training manager with eventually a substantial but not overloaded (at that time) team of trainers, I was charged with developing a management training structure for an organization that was in a high state of change and in which the prior management training had been minimal and largely ineffective (I had experienced this first hand as one of the managers!).

My early role in taking this post was that of consultant, involved in the diagnosis and analysis of training needs and presenting this analysis in the form of recommendations for acceptance by the organization. The approach recommended and eventually agreed on suggested a change from a management training event that included just about everything and taught little to a series of knowledge and skills modules. These modules did not exist in any form at that stage, so my first role change was to become a training course module designer assisted by a small group of trainers. Once designed, the modules were gradually introduced and I acted as a trainer on the new modules, while continuing the design role and also taking on an increasing management role. Once the earlier modules had been introduced and were becoming established, I withdrew from the direct training role and substituted another trainer who had been recruited and trained in the meantime. So again I was back to a strong management role with the team of trainers performing the training functions on my behalf. I did, however, maintain an element of direct training in one or two modules where my particular skills were necessary and appropriate and where further diagnoses were necessary, not only of subjects required, but also of the potential trainee population.

Finally, with a full complement of trainers (in addition to a capability to engage external consultants on contract), I was virtually a manager pure and simple, although I still indulged in some of the training activities that appealed to me!

This arrangement is not uncommon, and it meant I covered many roles in which training managers find themselves more or less permanently involved.

As a training manager of whatever nature, the questions that arise in the assessment of trainer effectiveness, apart from those directly related to trainer skill, are concerned with attitudes. Is the trainer operating in the general role required by the organization? Is the trainer seen as committed to the required role? Is the training manager in tune with what is required by the organization? Does the training manager know which role the trainer is playing?

And, as importantly, does the training manager know what role he is playing and at what time. The role the training manager is involved in can shift dramatically within a short span. He can be the developer of curricula at one point, a trainer next, and again the manager. This creates, especially as it relates to his management role, a clear need to understand the specific role he is playing at the particular time. For instance, if a trainer is being judged on training material developed by the training manager doing the evaluation, the manager must eliminate his own bias resulting from his personal involvement in the development of the material.

Assessment of trainer effectiveness involves not only the examination of the trainer's skills by the training manager and the trainer (and, as we shall see, by others), but also a questioning of the value of each general role within the organization. Assessment all too often considers the skill aspect only.

The descriptions of the various trainer roles demonstrates the care necessary in allocating a title to a "trainer" or training function. Even the role descriptions given here are not universally applied—for example, *trainer* is often seen as identical to *instructor*. When assessment is involved, however, it is the role, not the title, that should be recognized and understood.

Chapter Three

The Skills of the Effective Trainer

Although other factors are important, it is the trainer skills that are in question when assessing the overall capability of the trainer. What are these skills? Burgoyne and Stuart produced a list of what they considered to be the skills required for a management trainer.[1] The following description of trainer skills is based on this list, amended on the basis of my own research with trainers from all sorts of disciplines and organizations and supplemented from my experience as a developing trainer.

ORGANIZATIONAL KNOWLEDGE

Knowledge about the organization or company varies according to whether we are considering an internally or externally based trainer. The internal trainer must be very aware of the organization/company role and products or service, the policies that dictate the day-to-day operation, and the developing projects. He must know the power structure within the organization, and from that the potential power of the people under training—how powerful are they, where are they placed in the hierarchy and where are they likely to go, what is their potential power, and so on. The vast majority of organizations have either internally developed and enforced procedures and rules and/or externally enforced regulations, such as health and safety regulations. These and any other functional procedures must be known by the trainer so the training messages do not conflict with such rules. Many training recommendations concern the deployment and use of resources and people. Credibility can be lost if the

---

[1] John G. Burgoyne and Roger Stewart, *Personnel Review* 5, no. 4 (1976).

trainer recommends practices that are inconsistent with the availability of these resources.

The external training provider, who is also a contender for effectiveness assessment by the client, is in a more difficult position. Every attempt must be made both before and during the training event to obtain as much information about procedures and rules as possible. Real skill is often necessary to obtain this information while training is proceeding. The apparent skill and credibility of the provider are reduced each time a lack of knowledge becomes apparent.

MANAGEMENT ROLES AND FUNCTIONS

A further element of knowledge, linked with the previous skill, is concerned with the extent of the managerial role in the organization. What is the range of the manager's role? What are the extents and limits of responsibility and authority? What are the lines of reporting and what levels of resources are available to them? Is a particular management role any different from similar role titles in other departments, parts of the company, or other organizations? How free are managers to develop their organizational roles or do constraints restrict the desire to change? Is there a "management image" in the company and to what extent do the managers in the training population fit this image?

TRAINING KNOWLEDGE

Training knowledge must include familiarization with the academic and theoretical models and concepts applicable to training. The trainer must have a wide knowledge of training techniques, methods, and approaches to put these models into practice and a good appreciation of the circumstances in which each is the most appropriate. As discussed in the previous section, the various "trainer" roles must be understood, and the trainer must be able to identify the appropriate one for a particular situation. Many training authorities expect the trainer to know not only the details of a model, but also the originators or developers of the model. Knowledge of models is sometimes looked on as an end in itself, rather than the means to trace back to what the originator really meant. Note that I do not use the word *inventor* because there is little in training that is invented; most is developed from other practices or commonsense applications.

PROGRAM PREPARATION SKILLS

Most trainers, at some stage in their careers, have to consider design and prepare a complete training program that will satisfy the identified needs of the organization or individuals/groups within the organization. Program preparation requires skills in drawing together the material necessary for the event; selecting the most appropriate; putting it into a coherent, logical, and progressive order; and arranging its presentation in manageable sessions.

Decisions have to be made on the most appropriate way to present different parts of the program—an input presentation session, a discussion, a role-play or activity, use of a video, interactive video, or a computer program. Other decisions include whether parts of the program would be more effectively dealt with outside the event in an open learning approach or as a self-learning package. Many training contents can be approached in a number of ways, and skill is required in deciding the most effective approach considering the training population, the subject, the remainder of the event, the skills of the trainers, and so on.

SENSITIVITY TO PROGRAM FEEDBACK

Too many trainers are oblivious to the reaction of the learners as the training event is proceeding. The trainer must remain aware throughout the event, being sensitive to the behavior and direct or indirect feedback from the learners. Specific activities may be included to encourage this feedback; often, learners may have strong feelings about the training or the trainer but are unwilling or unable to feed these feelings back to the trainer.

For example, when I run a weeklong interpersonal skills course, at the start of the third, fourth, and fifth days I offer a feelings review that allows a continuous check on the participants' attitudes. I invite the participants to write down and then discuss as openly as possible three words that express their feelings at that point. This can often serve as a release valve for some pent-up feelings and the discussion can be traumatic. As with any solicited feedback, the trainer must be willing to accept this feedback and deal with whatever problems might emerge.

PEOPLE SKILLS

The principal skill of a trainer is not the ability to accumulate knowledge, but to communicate this knowledge to other people. He must ensure the information is understood and remembered by the trainees and that they are capable of both acting on the information and recall. Whatever the personality of the trainer, his behavior must be helpful to the learners. If the behavior is such that the learners dislike the trainer, the material presented must be very powerful to overcome this antipathy, which may affect the training or the likelihood the training will be implemented in the workplace after the training.

A wide variety of people skills is required. When delivering an input session, the skills of effective presentation are to the forefront, linked with an awareness of verbal and nonverbal signals that inform the trainer of the extent to which the material is being received. When input is linked with discussion and questioning, the additional skills of presenting "good" questions, listening to the responses, encouraging contributions, and probing to ensure understanding also come into play.

In group activity, the trainer must be capable of dealing with a number of different people at the same time, of allowing them to interact without interruption, and of knowing when and how to intervene using an appropriate type of intervention. Again, when using games, exercises, roleplays, and activities, other skills are used or added. The trainer must be skilled in presenting the activity information, content, or process and must be able to leave the groups alone when they are taking part (even if they are going wrong). And the trainer must have strong skills of eliciting feedback after the events.

The trainer, particularly the new trainer, must always remember he is in a position of power. I have often been surprised when comments or statements made much earlier in a training event are quoted back at me—"On x day at y o'clock, you said . . ."! From this power position, there is an opportunity to influence, and this must be used for the benefit of the learners, even to the extent that it can sometimes be used deliberately to model or encourage certain attitudes or behaviors.

The temptation to play games with people who are in a less powerful position than the trainer can sometimes be overwhelming. But this feeling must be resisted, because apart from being morally wrong, a backfire can easily occur when the learners realize what is being done to them. Remember that behavior, the most powerful human attribute in dealing with others, breeds behavior—what you do to me, I will do to you!

RESILIENCE

The trainer's function is not to influence people by making friends; training is not a popularity contest. Some trainers become upset if they do not become one of, if not the most popular one in, the group and employ all sorts of tactics to ensure this happens, even if the behavior is not congruent with the needs of the training. If the trainer concentrates on the training and the needs of the learner, there will be occasions when the trainer is far from popular. He must be capable of dealing with this, particularly if the "unpopularity" has been fostered for the sake of the learning.

In many facilitative situations, the trainer, who will be acting as an observer, will see the group digging holes for itself, following false trails, allowing itself to be dominated by one of the members, and so on. The temptation can be strong to help them get out of their difficulties (and at the same time receive their gratitude); this is usually the wrong action because the group needs to learn to solve its own problems.

Stress is not the prerogative of the learners who imagine (they tell me!) the trainers are superhuman and can cope with whatever is thrown at them. On the contrary, if the trainer is concerned about the success of his training, he will be under even more stress than the learners—he will have the stress of the situation itself as well as the stress of not letting this show to the learners. There will also be situations when it may be advisable for the trainer to let his stress emerge in view of the group—yet another decision skill!

When the trainer has to play a role or roles that are foreign to him, he is under a different kind of pressure, which again he may not show. All these and other situations make the role of the trainer particularly difficult because they are supplementary to the normal pressure of being in the training position. Faced with these stresses, the trainer must have emotional and behavioral resilience because he is often not in a position to deal immediately with the internal stress.

COMMITMENT

Commitment to the training and development of other people, to the organization to ensure the training is performed effectively, to producing learning events at the most effective level, and to developing skills to a stage where these other activities are possible is essential for the trainer. Without commitment, the training suffers in a myriad of ways. The absence of enthusiasm and sincerity to sell a new idea or method is quickly realized by the learners and reflects in their reactions. Learners excuse many faults and failings in their trainers when they recognize their enthusiasm, interest, and commitment, but the reverse also applies.

The organization must not expect this commitment as a right. Many trainers are appointed within an organization and can become a "trainer" with no initial enthusiasm. The commitment and enthusiasm of fellow trainers and the intrinsic interest and excitement of training often change the attitudes of these initial nonbelievers. Not all are affected in this way, however, and for those, every day of training must be a pain or a terror. Not everyone is interested in, capable of, training, and if this shows, and it surely will, the quicker the individual is out of training the better for him, the clients, and the organization.

MENTAL AGILITY

Training is a lively, active, and constantly changing area. Although little in the way of techniques and methods is new, the methods of presentation and production are always developing—or at least changing. To learn all the techniques and methods and to keep up with developments to be able to use them in an appropriate and effective way requires an inquiring and agile mind.

The days of the training lecture session in which the trainer controlled completely the content, level, and extent of the material are over, apart from perhaps the strictly procedural forms of training. The trainer has to be ready and able to answer penetrating and advanced questions by drawing on a sound knowledge. Credibility is easily lost by too often having to say you do not know the answer but will find out and report back. This must happen on occasion—you cannot know everything—but when it becomes the norm, something is wrong.

CREATIVITY

Modern training is not the presentation of what has always been presented in the way it has always appeared—"This subject has always been taught from a lecture so. . . ." The effective trainer must constantly be seeking new and realistic material and different ways of conveying information, not just for the sake of difference, but also for increased effectiveness.

These demands require the trainer to be aware of what is happening elsewhere and to consider how these other approaches can be used, modified or not, in the existing training. Awareness of a variety of training techniques and methods will almost certainly create different ways in which a feature can be improved. Creativity is necessary and to be applauded, but there is nothing wrong in taking existing approaches and changing them for your own purposes, particularly if the new way is an improvement on the old.

As an example of this type of modification, two particular activities are described in *50 Activities for Developing Management Skills.*[2] Both these activities are modifications of the "Report Activity." In one variation, a group activity designed to demonstrate planning, behavior planning, effective group working, negotiation, and conflict handling has three basic steps:

1. The production, in two separate groups, of a report comparing two opposing activities or points of view (e.g., group versus individual problem solving).
2. A planning period in which each group plans its strategy, as a group and individuals, for how to perform the one-to-one negotiations that will form the third stage.
3. The third stage in which each individual from a group meets face to face with an individual from the other group to negotiate the allocation of points between the two reports.

The third stage may be replaced by a joint meeting of the two groups to allocate the points between the reports. Both cases include feedback and discussion of the task results and processes that led to these. Both these

---

[2]Leslie Rae, *50 Activities for Developing Management Skills*, vol. 1 (Hampshire, England: Gower, 1988).

activities are susceptible to a number of variations of attitude, timing, and so forth, and on one occasion I produced a third variant I have found to be very effective. I was working in an area of change and needed to provide an activity that included this factor. There was not time to produce a custom-built activity, so both the "Report" variations were used—with a twist. The groups were started on the first stage with the information they would eventually be engaging in the one-to-one negotiations. About two thirds of the way through the first stage, two members from each group were exchanged—a first element of change. During the second stage, with about five minutes to go before the negotiations were due to start, the groups were told individual face-to-face meetings were not possible, so they would have to meet as one group—a second element of change. In many cases, changes introduce aspects of conflict and provide considerable material for discussion.

SELF-DEVELOPMENT

Hand in hand with many of the other skills come the ability and the commitment to improve one's own skills. It is often easy to plan, advise on, inform, and process the development of others, but much more difficult when you have to do this for yourself. This process involves both knowledge and skill and is essential for the trainer in keeping abreast of training developments and ensuring development within the profession.

As in most occupations and professions, training and trainers cannot stand still. Although there is little new in training, trainers must keep up to date with the developments of the existing material, different ways of using it, and so on. Also, they must be aware of and able to learn about new products—films, videos, computer programs, interactive video, equipment such as black whiteboards, automatic printing whiteboards, and OHP slide producers.

The knowledge content includes self-awareness of your own behavior and its effects, so you might engage in behavior modification to improve your training effectiveness.

If there is more than one form of training in your organization, it is in your interests to learn more about these other areas and so increase the size of your personal trainer's tool kit.

If training, as so often happens, is looked on as a useful stage in the progression of a career-minded person, you need to find out optimum time in training from a career point of view, and ensure you have the necessary qualifications or knowledge to advance when your time to move on arrives.

One of the indicators of future success is the desire to develop to the fullest extent possible, even if this means self-activity. An intent self-developer will almost certainly be a high achiever at any stage of his career.

The uninterested trainer will usually be seen as ineffective. If an individual trainer has either no skill or no interest in his own effectiveness, he could be doing considerable training damage. However, the trainer who keeps on asking himself and others, "How am I doing?" has a much greater opportunity of determining his effectiveness and whether and what he needs to improve.

As in any aspect of work, feedback to others on their behavior and general communication triggers the behavior-breeds-behavior syndrome and prompts return feedback.

Self-awareness in the trainer is not only valuable in assessing training effectiveness, but it also provides insight into the trainer's own emotions, values, beliefs, assumptions, and judgments.

It is often said by trainers that there are good courses and bad groups. Usually, the trainer is blind to a lack of skill on his part when he fails to achieve success, and he consequently blames the group. The belief that learners are becoming less skilled in benefiting from training may imply a diminution in the trainer's skills—again a failure of awareness.

Effective trainers must be aware of their value judgments and their possible effects on their training, such as attitudes toward equal opportunities, sex differences, and race, color, political, and religious differences. It is not wrong for trainers to have personal views and internal attitudes about any of these, but they must be very aware of these feelings and ensure they are not letting them intrude on their training performance.

SHARING

The effective trainer is rarely one who works alone as a deliberate method of operation, although sometimes this is forced on an individual. Awareness and development are desirable attributes for an effective trainer, and these are virtually impossible in a closed situation. Aware trainers may think they can assess the results of their own behavior, but these assessments can be wildly inaccurate without feedback from others. Knowledge can be accumulated in isolation—reading books, watching films and videos, using computer programs—but so much of our learning is from others. We can observe alternative approaches, sound out our ideas and innovations, and keep up to date on movements with which we might otherwise not be aware. Training is a "people" job in so many ways, and the more contact with people, the greater the likelihood there is of the trainer having a wider and more enlightened outlook.

CREDIBILITY

If learners are to notice the messages you are trying to convey, you must present a credible image. This can be achieved by:

- Being charismatic despite limited knowledge.
- Being charismatic in company with extensive knowledge.
- Being seen as an "expert" or very experienced person in the subject.
- Having effective training skills.
- Having a behavioral pattern that does not offend the learners.
- Having a willingness to demonstrate that you can and want to learn yourself.
- Not projecting yourself as the "expert."

Visible timidity and uncertainty tend to reduce credibility, particularly with some types and levels of learner, as does a demonstration of lack of knowledge of the subject. Credibility can also be reduced if the trainer behaves unacceptably—criticizing in public members of the group, denying individual and group needs and rights, and failing to carry out promised actions. During one training course in which I was a student, the first three hours were spent, at the invitation of the trainers, in determining our specific needs. After this activity, which raised our expectations considerably, our reported needs were simply ignored and the trainers proceeded with their predetermined training program. Both trainers and the training immediately lost any credibility in our eyes, to the extent that several of the learners left the event as soon as they saw what was happening.

Although the trainer holds initially a position of power over the group (whether sought or not), this can quickly dissipate if it is abused, with a loss of credibility.

HUMOR

In general, learning is more likely to be effective if the atmosphere in which it is conducted can be lightened at relevant times by some form of humor. This does not mean the trainer must have an inexhaustible supply of jokes, nor that the amount of learning equates with the amount of laughter emanating from the training room. An over-solemn approach can inhibit learning in many people, however, because the situation becomes too stressful. On the other hand, too lighthearted an environment can be unhelpful to learning, although it may be enjoyable.

A case in point is the attitude of different people toward the various approaches in available videos. Some of these feature well-known performers who create a great deal of laughter. Other productions approach the subject with less well-known, but equally capable actors using a more serious approach. Of course, there are shades in between.

Many people prefer the first type, saying they learn because they notice the well-known performer and/or because the humor eases the situation and thus encourages learning. Many people take the opposite view in that they are distracted by the well-known cast and the laughter gets in the way of the "serious" business of learning. This is one of the problems faced by the trainer when groups of "mixed" learners are present at the event—and they are almost invariably mixed in a variety of ways. You cannot satisfy all the learners all the time, so some form of compromise must be accepted.

To be effective, humor must be unforced and relevant, because forced humor is usually obvious and fails to be funny, and irrelevant humor can result in loss of credibility—"Why on earth did he tell that story?" Humor must not be forced when the trainer is not a humorous person, although with practice and experience even this state can be improved. There are few things more capable of destroying a situation than a joke that fails.

Humor, however, need not be in the form of jokes. The recounting of a relevant, humorous incident in which you were involved, and preferably in which you were the victim, is often much funnier and seen as relevant humor. The effective trainer often builds up a bank of these anecdotes, which can be introduced at relevant points and often relieve an over-serious situation. Be careful of the "supplied" anecdotes that may be used by several trainers—learners often attend training events by different trainers, and if they hear the same anecdote recounted as a personal event by more than one trainer, they begin to be suspicious! It is important that humor support the point of the training. A humorous anecdote that demonstrates the point of the training will enhance its retention by the learner, while humor for humor's sake will diminish the retention.

Therefore, in presentation skills, humor is not an essential element, although it is often desirable and can give lighthearted relief if delivered in a natural and appropriate manner. Otherwise rely on knowledge, training skill, and a friendly behavior.

The effective trainer's sense of humor is not directed outward only. An effective trainer must have the ability to laugh at himself or lighten his emotions in some way, otherwise stress can build up to an unacceptable level. Every trainer has at some time had doubts about a number of things, had a "bad" course, and thought "that's it! I'm not putting myself through that anymore." It is often only resilience backed by a sense of humor that can pull someone out of this despondency—plus the knowledge that virtually every trainer goes through these emotions, not once in their careers, but usually many times.

SELF-CONFIDENCE

The final factor required in a trainer is confidence in the ability to transmit skills and knowledge to the learners. Many highly skilled and knowledgeable individuals are unable to act as trainers because they lack the confidence to stand up and impart their knowledge. The skills of presentation can be learned; the presentation content and method can be planned and prepared for; but still a gap can exist that holds the individual back from having the self-confidence to stand up in front of what is, in the vast majority of cases, a friendly group of people.

Have you as a trainer, or have your trainers, these extra apparent qualities? I say "apparent" because the confident approach and appearance need only be superficial, at least in the early stages. The external image may be of confident, relatively nerveless skill, but underneath the presenter is a quivering mass of jelly! It is to the apparent image that the learners will be reacting. Like most performers who admit to having huge butterflies before going on stage, the trainer experiences nerves because the trainer is also a performer and the session a performance. Most trainers need to start worrying when:

- They stop having stage fright symptoms, because this may mean they are no longer concerned about the level of performance they are about to give.
- The butterflies stay with them, and may even increase throughout the session, producing a less than effective performance.

If, however, you don't get nervous, do not worry that you are not a concerned trainer. Recently I heard a well-established actor say during a television interview that nerves did not affect him, and he couldn't understand why it should "because performing is my job, and if I'm not capable of performing it, I shouldn't be doing it." However, for most of us this is an extreme attitude.

ASSESSING THE SKILLS

The above descriptions detail 17 specific skills that are required in every trainer, particularly those engaged in the wider or more elevated aspects of training and development. But the 90 percent (at least) of us who cannot claim effectiveness in all or most of the skills must not give up hope. Learners excuse many aspects of a trainer's failings. Some degree of most of the skills must be present to produce a reasonably effective trainer, and absence of many must raise serious doubts about the person's ability to train effectively.

Most of the skills are observable and/or assessable, or at least the apparent behavior related to the skills, and it is the observable behavior that matters in most cases.

Skills alone do not make a trainer. Trainers are human beings and consequently differ from each other and the norm to a considerable extent. In a meaningful assessment of trainers, it is therefore necessary to have some measure of the rich variety that exists.

Chapter Four

Trainer Functions

The intrinsic behavioral skills of an individual are not the only measures that can be applied to the trainer. In the previous chapter, we saw the various roles that might be demanded of a "trainer" because of the type of training in which he is involved. Trainers are people, however, and as such reflect a wide variety of types and attitudes. From these attitudes and their related overt behaviors, trainers can be placed into categories, which will help the assessor understand more fully the person he is assessing.

THE "TOWNSEND MODEL"

At a reasonable "tongue-in-cheek" level of assessment, we find a three-dimensional model proposed by John Townsend.[1] He suggests that trainers operate, and hence take on type roles, in three dimensions:

1. Competence and/or knowledge in the subject matter being taught.
2. Skills of teaching the subject matter, defined as:
   - Platform skills and other direct training skills.
   - The ability to put learning theory into practice.
   - The application of knowledge about adult learning.
   - The ability to design, prepare, and organize material effectively.
3. Concern centered on the needs of the learners.

Figure 4–1 presents the typology as a three-dimensional matrix with the above components as the identifying features. Within each category,

---

[1]John Townsend, "The Trainer Grid", *JEIT* 9, no. 3 (1985).

FIGURE 4–1
The Townsend Model

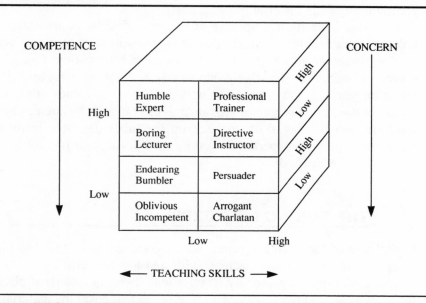

Source: *JEIT* 9, no. 3 (1985). MCB.

there must be some grading, so any category will have extreme, typical, and weakly represented members, in addition to a tendency toward a neighboring, related type. Teaching, as used here, is the ability to impart knowledge and skill to the learner.

THE HUMBLE EXPERT

The humble expert category of trainer has high competence, low teaching skills, and high concern.

The humble expert has an intimate knowledge of his subject and is, as the name implies, a recognized expert. It would be very easy for him to present his knowledge in a way that would leave his audience in no doubt about his expertise. Because of the high concern for people and their learning requirements, he is not likely to take that approach, but is more self-effacing and empathic. However, he does not have the training skills with which to capitalize on this approach, and consequently he is more likely to appear apologetic, obtuse, disorganized, and repetitive in the presentation of his material.

His value is easily lost because of the lack of skills in presentation, unless the learners recognize the golden opportunity they have and work hard to extract the gold nuggets from this mine of information. It requires a very committed or sensitive group to take this action, a group that is intent on learning and does not mind what it does to achieve this. If a trainer of this nature is recognized, amends can be made by attempting to instill in him training skills to back up the other desirable qualities. Sometimes the very expertise is getting in the way, and this difficulty must also be addressed.

THE BORING LECTURER

In the case of the boring lecturer, we have the category that has high competency, but both low teaching skills and low concern.

This is the typical university lecturer who dwelt in cloistered circles for many years and has produced a set of briefs that cover the material to be presented and uses these, almost unamended, for the rest of his career. Although this is a stereotype, examples exist, and not only in the hallowed halls. Industrial and commercial training has its share of them. Usually they are to be found in environments where there is high technological input into the training, and they may be the highly qualified professional. In many cases, they are not full-time trainers but are the guest speaker, introduced into an event because

- They are the experts in the organization.
- They are highly placed in the organization and "like to support training."
- They are used to fill an empty space in the training program.
- If the trainer had to take the subject session, he would have to prepare for it.

In many cases, it is not the boring lecturers' fault that they fall into this category. Sometimes they are fully aware they are the experts, and in front of a group of learners, they can't be bothered with the cosmetics of training techniques; those people are here to learn and here is the message from the expert's mouth. The developmental needs of an individual of this nature are much greater than of the humble expert. Training skills can be taught once the individual becomes aware of his shortcomings. There are also the questions of attitude and concern for the learners. If the skills of training are accepted, relationship to the learners may be a spin off from this training. Awareness is not always as easily introduced, particularly in some of the more remote people who may not even accept that they are low in training skills or may believe training skills are not even necessary.

THE ENDEARING BUMBLER

Almost at the other end of the scale from our two experts who have little or no concern for people, the endearing bumbler is represented by low competence and low teaching skills but high concern for people.

The endearing factor about this person is that, although he may approach his training tasks in a confused, disorganized, incompetent way, he is very concerned that he is dealing with people who are learners and who are seeking help and guidance. Training events involving this type are likely to contain long lunch and refreshment breaks and may vary considerably from the program because the trainer is very aware of the learners' needs (whether or not these relate to what should be taught) and reacts to these needs. Consequently, despite the bumbling, the delegates may learn something. However, this type of trainer, delightful though he may be as a person, needs to be taken in hand and introduced not only to training skills, but also to the need to prepare and have the relevant knowledge available. All this action must be taken without decreasing the concern for the people they have to train.

THE OBLIVIOUS INCOMPETENT

The all too common oblivious incompetent is characterized by low competence, low teaching skills, and low concern for people.

Somehow, they have entered the training field, have probably read a lot about knowledge and skills, without realizing what they meant, and have concluded they are highly skilled as trainers. Their false image of themselves blinds them to the fact that the learners are learning nothing—end-of-course validation sheets that give this message are brushed off as coming from a very poor group.

> "Happiness sheets" tell you nothing. I didn't set out to be popular. The end-of-course sheets are asking the wrong questions or the group has misunderstood what was being asked. They just weren't bright enough to see the models, concepts, analogies I was presenting to them.

There are two basic ways to approach trainers of this type. They can be told of their failings by someone senior to them who they recognize as being a skilled expert and, if they accept the truths, can benefit from both skills and attitude training. Or they can be transferred to where they do not have to be concerned about people and conveying information or skills, and where they can make direct use of whatever skills they might have.

THE ARROGANT CHARLATAN

The arrogant charlatan is an interesting combination of low competence, high teaching skills, and low concern for people.

The principal motivation of this type of trainer is to present himself as a skilled trainer, slick in presentation and demonstration, giving the learners an exposition from which they should not be able to fail to learn. This attitude is based on the belief that you do not need to know the subject on which you are training, as long as you have learned all that is necessary for the session. The brief has been learned by heart or is a detailed written document that is followed slavishly; and the stage management notes are all carefully annotated—when to tell a joke, and which one, when to show a visual aid. The visual aids are usually superb, because they have been copied from the original source—not necessarily with understanding—or have been prepared by someone else with real skill.

The biggest problem this type of trainer has during a session is trying to fend off insistent questioning about material that is not covered by the brief. In this case, the arrogance simply sweeps away or ignores the questioning. Although the learners may initially be impressed by the apparent skill, the credibiity gap soon becomes evident as the learners realize the limited extent of the knowledge and concern for their learning.

The remedies are again confrontation, followed by assistance with developing the people relationship factors and understanding the needs of the learners. The needs aspect will reflect the competence level, which can be improved by a more realistic approach to preparation—the trainer should aim to have a wider knowledge than is necessary in the basic session brief. With a demanding learner group, knowledge is not the only essential; there must also be the knowledge/skill/adeptness to relate problems presented by the learners to the training and to real life. Consequently, there must be a real understanding of what is being presented.

THE PERSUADER

The characteristics of the persuader are those of low competence, high teaching skills, and high concern.

Many trainers fall into this category, particularly those corporate trainers who have to cover an extremely wide range of subjects. In such cases, the competence (i.e., knowledge and skills of a subject) may be relatively low because they have to take on so many subjects, in many of which they will not have had firsthand working experience. Yet the organization requires them to train others in the subject. All they can do, particularly if time is short, is to learn as much as they can about the subject from books, experts, and practitioners. From this they will have to produce a satisfactory working brief, but with the awareness that the learners' demands may exceed this knowledge.

The principal difference between the persuader and the charlatan is that the former has sufficient concern for the learners to admit openly this failing, but to take positive action to find out and report back whatever the learners want to know.

To succeed, the persuader must have an extensive and relevant knowledge of training and learning techniques to ensure the learners obtain as much as possible from their intervention. The persuader uses these techniques because he wants to help the learners rather than because he wishes to demonstrate his own skill or give the learners only what he wants to give them.

In many ways, the trainer who acts as a facilitator of learning, rather than operating in a teaching mode, is a persuader who does not really need to have an in-depth knowledge of procedures and methods within the subject. He is there to help the learners come to terms with the learning using their own resources. Obviously, so much the better if the facilitator also has the detailed competence, but at times this is either not possible or even necessary. The external provider of training is often in this situation.

THE DIRECTIVE INSTRUCTOR

We have already encountered a role description of the directive instructor, but if we look at inherent knowledge, skills, and attitudes, the type has high competence and high teaching skills, but a lower concern for the learners.

Much corporate training relates to the clerical, procedural, technical, and technological skills required for the employees of the organization to be able to perform their tasks and duties. Fewer organizations look to the wider training needs of supervisors and managers at all levels in their less specific roles.

The directive instructor usually trains using a set manual or training procedure that rarely allows much in the way of variation in either content, structure, or timing. If the learners' needs differ in any way from the syllabus of the training event, little is done, not because the instructor is not supportive to these needs, but because the course has to be run according to his directive. Often this is the correct way to go about the training—there is a set procedure for doing a job and this must be taught so this method and procedure is learned.

The unfortunate aspect of this type of trainer is that they have usually operated in the same way for so long that when circumstances suggest a different approach will be more effective they are unable to change. If the instructor is in a training environment that demands instruction, well and good; if he is still an ''instructor'' in a rapidly changing environment that demands varied approaches, there can be many problems.

THE PROFESSIONAL TRAINER

The professional trainer may be the ideal trainer type for all forms of training, except direct instruction described above. The characteristics of someone who fits this type are high competence, high teaching skills, and high concern for people.

The word *professional* is used in its widest, supportive sense. This type of trainer has wide knowledge, experience, and understanding of a range of subjects; has detailed knowledge of a wide variety of training techniques, methods, and applications and knows when to use each one to the most effective result; and has a strong concern for the learners. In his relationship with the learners, he can handle people in groups, large or small, face to face, formal or informal situations, and he is not averse to discussing, advising, even counseling out of training hours, perhaps in meal or refreshment breaks.

There is always the danger that he will become too good, or be seen as such, but this should be less of a danger than in some of the other types because of this skill and real concern for the learners.

How are these "super-trainers" identified? Perhaps the principal evidence is the apparent absence of stress in the trainer and a real absence of stress in the learners; an acceptance of the trainer in any situation by the learners (although he need not top the popularity polls); the readiness of the trainer to answer truthfully questions from the learners (and this includes the willingness to disclose a lack of knowledge, but a similar willingness to find out); a readiness to learn from the learners; a visible need to help the learners to learn and transfer their learning to their real-life needs; and, above all, a positive and optimistic attitude toward life and learning, practicing what he preaches, thus demonstrating the training messages do not originate in an unrealistic ivory tower.

Although Townsend's trainer type titles may appear lighthearted, they nevertheless represent the main types found among trainers, not necessarily because of the organizational role in which they have been cast, but because that is their preferred approach to training. Perhaps the real mark of the professional trainer is his ability to be flexible and perform in some of the other roles as the occasion arises, without complaining that this is not the type of training he prefers.

The only category of Townsend's that I have altered is the persuader. Townsend called him the "shallow persuader." I believe this was too harsh a name for what is the enforced and preferred role of many trainers—I know that I have been in this role more than once.

LEARNING STYLES

The discussion about the trainer roles suggested by Townsend referred to trainers' typology being the result of their professional preferences—I want to be impressive; I want to help these learners; I must make sure that they learn the regulations. Trainers (people) may be considered in terms of their preferred approach. David Kolb in the United States pioneered the approach of categorizing people according to their preferred ways of learning, and this work has been continued in a modified way in

Britain by Alan Mumford and Peter Honey in their "Learning Styles." Learning is part of life, and I believe that the preferences shown for learning in "Learning Styles" are reflected in a much wider context of how we prefer to (and often do) behave.

The preferences in the Honey and Mumford "Learning Styles" are obtained by completing a questionnaire or inventory that consists of 80 statements with which the respondent has to agree or disagree, whether the statement refers to them or not, by entering a check or a cross. Typical statements are:

I have strong beliefs about what is right and wrong, good and bad.

I am attracted to more novel, unusual ideas than to practical ones.

I am careful not to jump to conclusions too quickly.

I am keen to reach answers via a logical approach.

I can often see better, more practical ways to get things done.

The responses are scored by totaling the number of checks; that is, the number of statements with which the learner agrees. Honey and Mumford have identified four main learning preference styles: activists, reflectors, theorists, and pragmatists.

Activists are people who prefer to learn by doing something, even at times simply for the sake of doing it. They revel in innovative approaches, but having introduced the innovations tend to become bored with them and start looking for new fields. They are either the ones who jump in first when something has to be done or else they sit fuming, thinking, "Why don't they just get on with it instead of rabbiting on!" Watch the activist trainer when he has given the training group a task to perform or an inventory to complete or has asked them to reflect on some aspect of the training. After the first minute, it usually becomes obvious he doesn't know what to do with himself while the others are working! One can almost see him thinking: "Why don't they get on with it? Why are they taking so long? Should I walk around the room or should I leave the room until they've finished?"

Reflectors are interested in learning new concepts and practices but prefer to sit back and think about the implications and possible actions before saying or doing anything. They like to consider tasks and problems from all angles and are cautious before making a move. Often they are the very quiet members of the group, and before they can come out with the results of their deliberations, the activists have burst in and pressured everybody into doing something—right or wrong. Reflectors can become very annoyed with the activists who are interrupting their reflective processes, but the reverse does not necessarily apply. In fact, the activist is so busy "doing" that he may not even notice the reflectors reflecting!

Theorists are also in many respects reflectors, but their reflections are much deeper, and they insist on knowing, comparing, and understanding the basic data, the assumptions, and the theories and models on which the ideas are based. They are the logical, rational, and objective thinkers who like to consider everything before reaching a decision. The basic criterion on which they work is "If it can't be explained, I don't want to know." Learning is limited if sufficient time is not given for them to consider, discuss, and argue the possibilities and in doing so will certainly annoy the activists and may even annoy the reflectors who want some quiet to consider their own thoughts. It is common for people with a strong theorist preference to have either an equally strong or moderately strong reflector preference.

Pragmatists are the practical people who are interested in trying out new ideas, but only if it is shown they have a practical, working value with specific and direct applications in the workplace. The subjective attitudes of the activists are not for them. They are usually hardworking, fully involved people when a problem has to be solved or a task to be completed, but they can disturb other preference types by their insistence on practical application.

It would be dangerous to attempt to apply a single label to individuals, particularly where the choice is only between four dominant types. The Learning Styles approach recognizes this, and people who complete the Learning Style questionnaire finish with scores in all four types. The distribution of these scores then becomes the important issue, and application of the questionnaire to several thousand individuals has determined statistical distribution levels.

Scores can be allocated within each style to preferences at very strong, strong, moderate, and weak levels, where the boundary between the moderate and the strong levels determines the influence of that particular type. If the scores are above the norm, the style takes on a real meaning in that individual's preference approaches, although the extent of the scoring also indicates the greater or lesser preference. For example, a score of about 11 or more in the activist style indicates the individual has a strong preference for that style; below that score, this style does not become too much of an influence in that individual's life. The scores for reflectors, theorists, and pragmatists have a norm with scores 14, 15, and 14, respectively.

These are the norms for a wide, heterogeneous population of managers and supervisors. Specific norms are being constructed for particular groups, such as training managers and sales managers, although some groups still have insufficient examples to ensure the profiles are valid.

Where individuals show strong or very strong preferences, there are a number of possible and usual permutations. People can have one style only as an "above the line" preference—activist, reflector, theorist, or pragmatist. Or there can be combinations of preferences—reflector and theorist, reflector and pragmatist, and reflector-theorist-pragmatist. Perhaps the ideal is if all the styles are represented in an individual's profile at about the norm level or slightly above. This suggests the individual is balanced and can utilize all the styles whenever the relevant occasion arises. There is usually a bias toward one or two styles. Occasionally, there are some strange bedfellows—the score indicates preferences in an individual for both activist and reflector. In most respects, these are contrasting styles and, if the questionnaire has been answered honestly and accurately, may suggest a conflict of interests and actions.

The four styles are linked directly with the four principal stages of the learning cycle in which total learning is achieved when something is done, experienced, actioned, and so forth. The experience is then considered in terms of what happened, when, how, by whom; and questions are asked, "Was that the only way to do it?" "What alternative approaches could have been taken?" "How many alternative approaches are there?" "Why did that happen/so and so do that?" When everything has been considered and all relevant information and learning extracted, plans can then be made about what should be done on the next occasion in similar situations. The cycle is completed by further action, which is then reviewed, and so on.

If an individual has a strong preference for one style only, there is the danger he may become locked in to one of the stages of the cycle and consequently not learn to the full extent.

IMPLICATIONS OF THE LEARNING STYLES FOR TRAINERS

If a trainer is locked in, albeit unconsciously, to a particular style, this attitude and preference will likely be reflected in the way he approaches his training function. The activist is more likely to design events in which much is happening, but may ignore the need to build in time for reflection. The theorist trainer may become too involved in the intricacies of the "hows" and the "whys" and manipulate complex discussions that many of the learners may find uninteresting.

The organization using the trainer may require a particular style to be employed. If the trainer easily reflects this style, there is no problem, but if the required style conflicts with the trainer's preferred style, difficulties may arise. It is the responsibility of the trainer assessor to be aware of both the trainer's preferences and the organizational requirements, in addition to considering the best training/learning practices.

A range of techniques is often needed to balance the type of learning necessary with the learning needs and preferences of the learners. This level of training demands trainers with wide-ranging preferences who are able to cope with changes in approach without letting their personal dominant preferences influence their work.

Conversely, in the instructor type of training, the very strong activist who is unable to control his preference can be an embarrassment and can diminish the impact of the structured learning.

The assessor must also be aware that, although preferences are an intrinsic part of an individual, the strong preferences can be controlled by a determined individual allowing weaker preferences to develop. A subsequent benefit of the assessment might be helping an individual's development, once his preferences and their implications have been recognized.

Learning styles and trainer styles are closely allied, and the assessor must recognize that a number of factors are at work in determining the trainer's role and function. Chapters 2, 3, and 4 have discussed some of the forces at work in forming these roles. The next chapter addresses instruments designed to help identify these various roles, functions, and preferences.

Chapter Five

Identifying Trainer Types

THE TRAINEE-CONTENT TRAINING INVENTORY: AN OVERVIEW

There are many different methods of considering the types and roles found among trainers and the ways in which they can meet the needs of the organization and the learner—our classical training trio. One of these, which has a direct relationship with both trainer attitudes and organizational attitudes, is known as the "Trainee-Content Training Inventory" (T-C Inventory).

This inventory compares the preferences, attitudes, and activities of trainers in two dimensions. The first is trainee orientation, which is concerned with the trainer's attitudes and awareness, reflecting an emphasis on sharing authority and responsibility with the trainees versus an emphasis on retaining authority in the training situation. The other dimension is content orientation in which the trainer's choice is emphasis on the job of the trainer—the performance of task activities including planning and scheduling course content and evaluating trainee progress versus emphasis on role attributes, having the respect of trainees and colleagues, being an expert, and evaluating trainee progress.

T-C TRAINING INVENTORY BACKGROUND

Both of the orientations exist simultaneously in the behavior of every trainer. A trainer can be highly trainee oriented and highly content oriented at the same time. A trainer's personal philosophy determines the emphasis he places on each orientation. Some trainers who believe the needs of trainees and the system are mutually exclusive and inevitably in conflict strive to resolve the problem by concentrating on one or the other set of needs. Other trainers, while also believing a conflict between incompatible needs is inevitable, work toward some compromise or balance in which neither orientation is fully emphasized. Still other trainers see the trainee orientation and content orientation as functionally related. They aim to integrate trainee and system needs by emphasizing both.

In completing the inventory, the following should be kept in mind:

1. Many of the items are repeated. This is not to test the consistency of the participants' responses, as is the case in many instruments, but to relate the possible choices to a variety of circumstances.
2. Participants may find it difficult to choose the "most important" statement of two equally attractive alternatives. The participant must choose one or the other.
3. Participants may find some items in which they believe both alternatives are unattractive. In such cases, a choice must still be made, perhaps the "least unattractive."
4. Completion is best when tackled quickly—the immediate gut feeling—because too much consideration tends to increase the thoughts of "Which is the best answer I should give?" rather than "What do I really feel?"

THE TRAINEE-CONTENT TRAINING INVENTORY[1]

The following questions concern your attitudes toward some training practices. Their purpose is to provide you with some indications for you to discuss about you as a trainer. There are no right or wrong answers: the best answer is the one most descriptive of your attitudes. Therefore, when answering the questions below, select the answer you feel to be true for you, as only realistic answers will provide you with useful information.

Each of the 40 items consists of two statements, either about what a trainer can do or how he can behave. Circle the letter A or B in front of the statement you think is the more relevant to your feelings. In the case of some of the items you may think that both alternatives are important, but you should try to choose the statement you feel is more important.

---

[1]The inventory is reproduced with permission from J. William Pfeiffer and John E. Jones, ed., *Annual Handbook for Group Facilitators* (San Diego: University Associates, 1974). It was originally titled "Student-Content Teaching Inventory."

Sometimes you may think that both alternatives are unimportant: you should still choose the statement you think is more important.

It is more important for trainers to:

1. A. organize their courses around the need and skills of every type of trainee.
   B. maintain definite standards of training performance.
2. A. let the trainees have a say in course content and objectives.
   B. set definite standards of training performance.
3. A. emphasize completion of the course program.
   B. let trainees help set objectives and content.
4. A. maintain trainees' progress by means of tests.
   B. allow trainees a voice in setting course objectives and content.
5. A. praise good trainees.
   B. allow trainees to evaluate the performance of their trainers.
6. A. allow trainees to make their own mistakes and learn from those experiences.
   B. work to cover the course subject matter adequately.
7. A. make it clear that they are the authority in the training situation.
   B. allow trainees to make their own mistakes and to learn from their experiences.
8. A. be available outside formal course hours to talk with trainees.
   B. be available during course hours only.
9. A. give tests to evaluate trainee progress.
   B. tailor the course content to match the needs and abilities of each group.
10. A. stay detached from the trainees.
    B. let trainees plan their own program according to their own interests.
11. A. take an interest in the trainees as people.
    B. make it clear that they are the authorities in the training situation.
12. A. stay detached from the trainees.
    B. be available outside formal course hours to talk with trainees.
13. A. modify their position if one of the trainees shows where they were wrong.
    B. maintain standards of performance.
14. A. allow trainees to have a say in evaluating performance.
    B. not socialize with the trainees outside course hours.
15. A. see that the group covers the prescribed subject matter for the course.
    B. be concerned about the trainees as people.
16. A. let the trainees learn by experience.
    B. maintain standards of training performance.
17. A. allow trainees a voice in setting course objectives and content.
    B. make it clear that they are the authorities in the training situation.
18. A. discourage unnecessary talking during training sessions.
    B. establish an informal atmosphere in the training situation.
19. A. allow trainees to evaluate the training.
    B. make it clear that the trainer is the authority in the training situation.
20. A. stay detached from the trainees.
    B. let the trainees make mistakes and learn by experience.

21. A. be an authority on the course materials.
    B. keep up to date in the field.
22. A. be regarded as a person of high technical skills.
    B. update course materials constantly.
23. A. attend to his/her own personal development.
    B. be an authority on the course materials.
24. A. attend to his/her own personal development.
    B. set an example for the trainees.
25. A. ensure that each trainee is working to his full capacity.
    B. plan, in detail, all training activities.
26. A. construct fair and comprehensive validation methods.
    B. set an example for his trainees.
27. A. be known as an effective trainer.
    B. ensure that each trainee is working to his full capacity.
28. A. construct fair and comprehensive validation measures.
    B. ensure that the trainee is getting something from the course.
29. A. be an authority on the subject matter.
    B. plan and organize their course work carefully.
30. A. be a model for the trainees to emulate.
    B. try out new ideas and approaches on the course/group.
31. A. ensure that each trainee is working to his full capacity.
    B. plan and organize the course content carefully.
32. A. be available outside formal course hours to talk with trainees.
    B. be an expert on the course subject matter.
33. A. set an example for the trainees.
    B. try out new ideas and approaches on the group.
34. A. teach on a variety of courses.
    B. be a model for the trainees to emulate.
35. A. plan and organize training activities carefully.
    B. be concerned with the way the trainees are reacting.
36. A. be an authority on the course content.
    B. be known as an effective trainer.
37. A. give tests and evaluate trainee progress.
    B. be an authority on the course materials.
38. A. read journals relevant to the subject.
    B. be respected as a person of high technical skill.
39. A. be respected for knowledge of course subject matter.
    B. try out new ideas and approaches on the group.
40. A. be an authority on the course content.
    B. construct fair and comprehensive validation measures.

T-C Inventory Scoring

1. Draw a line under item 20.
2. Items 1 to 20 comprise the T scale. Place an X next to each item for which you have chosen the response indicated below.

Item	Response	Item	Response	Item	Response
1	A	8	A	15	B
2	A	9	B	16	A
3	B	10	B	17	A
4	B	11	A	18	B
5	B	12	B	19	A
6	A	13	A	20	B
7	B	14	A		

3. Items 21 to 40, which comprise the C scale, are scored as above with the following answers

Item	Response	Item	Response	Item	Response
21	B	28	A	35	A
22	B	29	B	36	B
23	A	30	B	37	A
24	A	31	B	38	A
25	B	32	A	39	B
26	A	33	B	40	B
27	A	34	A		

4. The number of Xs scored for items 1 to 20 are counted:
   The number of Xs scored for items 21 to 40 are counted:

5. Next, both T and C scores should be plotted on the chart on the Summary Sheet. The score in the T box should be plotted on the left side (vertical scale) of the chart. The score in the C box should be plotted on the bottom (horizontal) scale of the chart. The participants make a mark where their T and C scores intersect.

T-C Inventory Scoring Chart

High
20

Strategy 2
Trainees do not really want to learn, but they will respond to trainers they like. The trainer's primary responsibility is to win trainees over so they can be taught.

Strategy 5
Trainees like all people learn and explore. A trainer's primary responsibility is to integrate trainee and system needs by creating a learning climate and making learning meaningful and relevant.

15

Strategy 4
Trainee and system needs are incompatible. It is of primary importance that something be taught, but trainee needs cannot be ignored. The trainer's first responsibility is to push them enough to get the work done but also to do something for them to maintain training session morale.

10

T 5

Strategy 3
Trainees are lazy and indifferent to learning. Since a trainer is helpless to change the situation, his primary responsibility is to present the information the system requires.

Strategy 1
Trainees do not want to learn, but they will respond to strong direction and control. A trainer's primary responsibility is to make sure the material gets taught.

0	5	10	15	20
Low		Content Orientation		High

THE T-C TRAINING INVENTORY: THE FIVE TRAINING STRATEGIES

Five pure training strategies (or styles) result from (1) the interaction of the trainee and content orientations and (2) the differing degrees of emphasis trainers place on each orientation. The five styles are discussed below and depicted on the scoring chart.

Strategy 1

The strategy at the lower right corner of the diagram defines the style of a trainer whose basic philosophy dictates that trainee and system needs are mutually exclusive. Thus, this trainer resolves the conflict by placing maximum emphasis on content orientation and minimum emphasis on trainee orientation.

For this trainer, the syllabus defines what should be (or perhaps what the organization has decreed). Since trainees may resist training and learning, the trainer's primary responsibility is to ensure material is taught. It is important to set definite standards of training performance and to check continually to see that trainees are meeting the standards. This is accomplished by giving frequent spot tests, attending all training session, and so on.

Strategy 2

This trainer, whose strategy appears at the upper left corner of the diagram, also believes trainee and system needs are incompatible and in conflict. Like his Strategy 1 colleague, this trainer believes trainees resist training and learning, but he disagrees that the basic conflict can be overcome by tight training session control. Instead, this trainer places maximum emphasis on trainee orientation and minimum emphasis on content orientation.

Trainees will learn from trainers they like—so being liked is both necessary and personally gratifying for this trainer. He believes a trainer's primary responsibility is to be supportive and to win the "friendship" of his trainees. This is accomplished by putting on a "good show" in the training session, ignoring attendance, allowing trainees to set their own course standards, socializing, and so forth.

Strategy 3

Like his Strategy 1 and 2 colleagues, the trainer whose strategy is defined in the lower left corner of the diagram also believes in the conflict of trainee and system needs and in trainees' resistance to learning. Unlike his colleagues, he feels helpless to deal with the situation. Trainees will learn what they want to learn, when they want to learn it. A trainer simply cannot change this. Thus, the trainer's primary responsibility is to present the information and follow his job description. If the trainer has a "good" group of trainees, he is lucky; if he has a "bad" group, there is nothing he can do about it. Those trainees with initiative and motivation will learn. For Strategy 3 trainers, their philosophy justifies mechanistic presentations. At the higher training level, these trainers may prefer to teach advanced seminars and shun the basic core courses.

Strategy 4

At the middle of the diagram is the strategy of trainers who believe in the basic incompatibility of trainee and system needs. They aim instead for a compromise, or balance, by fully emphasizing neither the trainee orientation nor the content orientation.

Both system needs and trainee needs matter, but these trainers cannot see how to put them together. They end up with a moderate level of concern for each. Thus, the system requires the trainers to give forms of testing, but they may specify the exact resources from which questions or tasks will be drawn, rather than using those decreed by the system.

Strategy 5

At the upper right corner of the diagram is the strategy of the trainer who believes that trainees are always learning. In the mind of this trainer, trainee and system needs are not inevitably in conflict. The aim is to integrate both sets of needs by placing maximum emphasis on both trainee and content orientations.

These trainers believe a trainer's primary responsibility is not to see that something is taught, but rather that something is learned. Thus, it is important to create a climate in which learning is meaningful and relevant. Learning activities are structured to bring maximum benefit to the trainee, the training system, and the trainer.

The preceding descriptions are clearly caricatures of trainer behavior; they are not intended to be descriptions of real people. There are as many different training strategies as there are trainers. The strategy descriptions exaggerate behaviors that differentiate types of trainers, not to simplify behavior but to make it more understandable. If the strategies are defined and people are aware of them, they can be changed.

The T-C Training Inventory is one way of opening this process by providing a vocabulary, a model, and experiences on which to focus one's own behavior.

TRAINER ROLE ORIENTATION

The T-C Training Inventory is but one of many instruments available to help trainers analyze their attitudes and preferences toward training. It would be simple to reproduce many of these, but that might not be helpful here. In addition to the "Learning Styles" analysis of Honey and Mumford and the T-C Inventory, I recommend the use of a third valuable instrument, the "Trainer Orientation Framework" constructed by Andrew Pettigrew.

Four predominant trainer types are identified by using this framework, based on their attitudes and orientations to work, and within this, two polarized factors are emphasized. The first relates to the orientation of trainers with respect to the way they present their material and relate to the learners.

At one extreme, the trainer sees training as similar to the traditional educational process in which courses are established based on the requirement to achieve set training objectives. Subject matter is researched thoroughly and developed for a formal and structured presentation to the learners. The course is seen as a mechanism for the transfer of knowledge, skills, and attitudes from the "expert" trainer to the learners. A very trainer-centered approach is developed that requires complete fulfillment of the training objectives determined before the program.

Alternatively, the trainer takes a much more flexible attitude and considers that he has the responsibility to determine the organizational needs and produce a training program that will satisfy them. Trainers in this mode will not be confined or contained in any way by the traditional approaches, rather they will be innovative and experimental and very sensitive to the needs and emotions of the learners. Programs approached in this style are very learner centered.

The other factors are concerned with the organization within which the training is performed. At one extreme, the trainer sees the training as maintaining the smooth running of the organization. Existing systems, procedures, technologies, and methods are there to be instilled in the learners because this is the corporate need. Problems and needs are addressed in a "fire-fighting" approach, as they arise.

At the other extreme, change is the paramount feature of the trainer's attitude. He sees training as the mechanism of change, changing the systems, procedures, technologies, and methods in an effort to make improvements. To this trainer type, training is not the only trainer function, but organizational needs and change must be assessed and anticipated, and the trainer is a principal agent in preparing other people for change.

The trainer's attitudes to these factors can be assessed or self-assessed and a role orientation identified. The general descriptions above relate to the extremes; positions will be taken on all points of the continuum.

TRAINER ORIENTATION QUESTIONNAIRE

The questionnaire approach suggested to identify the trainer orientation in this model is much simpler than that in the preceding inventory and other similar models. However, this simplicity is deceptive, for the user must think carefully about his attitudes, preferences, and practices before being able to answer the two questions. I am indebted to the Manpower Services Commission (now the Training, Enterprise and Education

FIGURE 5–1
Role Orientation

1. Do you have an orientation to the maintenance needs of your organization, that is, to ensuring the continuance of the existing activities, products, or services? Or do you have an orientation to bringing about change within the organization, that is, to ensure that training can respond to pressures for change from both outside and inside the organization to help it get geared up to meet new situations, objectives, etc. Mark on the scale below where you think you are.

| Maintenance orientation | | | | | | | | | | Change orientation |

```
...........................................................................
0    1    2    3    4    5    6    7    8    9    10
```

2. Do you have an orientation to traditional methods of training, that is, methods and approaches based on the education or "professional" model of training, based largely on classroom-based techniques and curriculum design? Or do you have an orientation to methods of intervention, that is, a "change agent" approach to training that involves greater participation in bringing about changes in systems, procedures, or technologies and in changing people's attitudes and approaches to work? Mark on the scale where you think you are.

| Traditional educational orientation | | | | | | | | | | Interventionist orientation |

```
...........................................................................
0    1    2    3    4    5    6    7    8    9    10
```

3. Now transfer the scoring information from 1 and 2 to the framework in Figure 5–1. Mark the place where both points coincide.

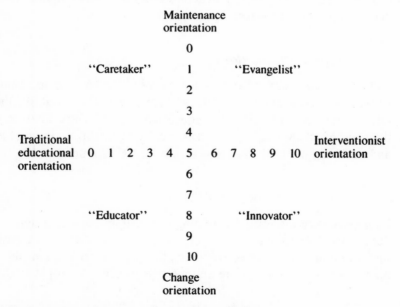

Source: *Guide to Trainer Effectiveness* (Moorfoot: MSC/ITD, 1984).

Division of the Department of Employment) and the Institute of Training and Development for this questionnaire, which appears in the *Guide to the Trainer Effectiveness.*[2]

Where the point is located on the framework indicates the preferred trainer role orientation, but it must be remembered that the emphasis of that role depends on the position within the quadrant, suggesting a typical extreme or "weak" member of that role and a close or distant relationship with other roles.

ROLE ORIENTATION: THE FOUR PREDOMINANT TYPES

Type 1: "Caretakers"

Caretakers see the need for training to maintain the smooth running of present systems, procedures, and technologies in the organization and adopt traditional educational approaches. They typically use trainer-centered approaches, highly structure programs, and respond to training needs as presented to them by someone in authority.

Type 2 "Educators"

Unlike the caretaker, educators see the need for training to change systems, procedures, and technologies in the organization, but like the caretakers tend to adopt traditional educational approaches. They anticipate the need for change and work strategically by setting training objectives and designing and scheduling appropriate training programs.

Type 3 "Evangelists"

Evangelists see the need for training to maintain present systems, procedures, and technologies in the organization, but they adopt a range of interventionist approaches. Basically, they believe traditional educational approaches are inappropriate and attempt to convert people in the orga-

---

[2]*Guide to Trainer Effectiveness* (Moorfoot: MSC/ITD, 1984).

nization to accepting a range of learner-centered experiences in the form of, say, workshops, seminars, and consultancy. They see their roles more as a facilitator of learning than an expert on the subject.

Type 4 "Innovators"

Innovators see the need for training to change systems, procedures, and technologies in the organization and adopt a range of interventionist approaches. They are particularly pervasive in the organization in order to understand the real needs that exist. They persuade people to become involved and guide them through a problem-solving process rather than proposing solutions. In essence, they are catalysts or change agents.

TRAINER TYPE INVENTORIES: THEIR USES

All the inventories and questionnaires described so far are principally for self-assessment and are invaluable for the trainer in assessing his own preferences and attitudes. However, they can have much wider use in the general area of trainer effectiveness assessment. The training manager assessing effectiveness can also use the inventories in a variety of ways.

In using any of these instruments in assessing trainees, the person conducting the assessment must understand his personal bias. Before an assessor can assess someone else, that assessor should have a good knowledge of his own attitudes, preferences, and beliefs. This knowledge will help the assessor recognize bias against the person he is assessing due to differences between them. For example, a training manager whose background has been very much in the instructor/theorist/educator roles and orientations may have difficulty assessing a trainer whose roles and orientations are much more toward the persuader/activist/innovator. If the assessor is aware of these differences and can identify the activities that relate to them, there is a much better likelihood of a fair assessment being made.

A complete knowledge, understanding, and awareness of the results of inventories and models such as these will help the assessor in these realistic assessments. Attitudes and preferences in themselves are insufficient for organizational and corporate assessment purposes, however. A trainer's effectiveness within an organization may depend on whether he meets the demands of the organization. There is little point in a trainer adopting the innovator role when the learning needs and the organizational culture demand an instructor approach. The trainer orientation and the organization needs must be congruent. If they are not, and this becomes evident in the assessments, several options are available.

- The trainer can accept that the needs of the organization are different from his own orientation, so he can and will adapt to the organizational requirements.

- The trainer can accept that the needs of the organization are different from his own orientation, so he can and will adapt to the organizational requirements but will steadily attempt to introduce changes that can be made acceptable to the organization and come nearer to his orientation.

- The trainer can accept that the differences exist, but realizes that the two requirements are not only incongruent but also that he cannot compromise his beliefs. Consequently, the only action is to terminate that employment and seek an organization that has a compatible structure.

There are alternative strategies, but all require compatibility between the trainer's current actions and the needs of the organization. This compatibility is what the assessor is assessing, whether we are considering self-assessment or manager assessment.

Chapter Six

The Uses of Training Validation

The skills of the trainer and the content of the training are inextricably intertwined. Both a training manager who has a number of trainers and observes them in action over a period of time and a learner who attends various courses with different trainers are aware of a mixture of effects. A good trainer with good material will produce a highly effective course; the same trainer with poor material will produce a poorer course, although not totally ineffective because his skill and experience will help to redeem the material. A poor trainer given good material will produce an ineffective learning experience, salvaged only perhaps by skilled learners who want to learn and do so despite the trainer; a poor trainer with poor training material gives the learners no chance.

So in addition to any assessment of the trainer's skills, the training material, its completeness, currency, necessity, and effectiveness must be reviewed. In many cases, this assessment must be subjective because of the nature of the training; in others, objective tests and examinations can be applied.

Every occupation and industry has its own jargon to describe its terms and processes. In training, the words *validation* and *evaluation* and even *assessment* are commonly used, although this is complicated by their conflicting use.

General dictionaries do not help much, being vague in their definitions. To validate is to "make valid (sound, defensible, well-grounded), ratify, confirm." To evaluate is to "ascertain amount of, find numerical expression for, appraise, assess" and even "determine the value of." Assessment is "the act of assessment, fixing the value of, a valuation" (usually applied in general dictionaries to a form of monetary valuation).

Within the professions interested in these subjects, there is little consistency. Some psychologists and trainers use the three words in an interchangeable way; others use one of them to mean all three effects; some have specific definitions that are in direct conflict with the definitions of others!

Some years ago, the British Manpower Services Commission attempted to produce a standardized glossary of training terms. My own approach is to accept these as effective working definitions.

The MSC definitions for *validation* are:

1. Internal validation. A series of tests and assessments designed to ascertain whether a training program has achieved the behavioral objectives specified.

2. External validation. A series of tests and assessments designed to ascertain whether the behavioral objectives of an internally valid training program were realistically based on an accurate initial identification of training needs in relation to the criteria of effectiveness adopted by the organization.

If these definitions are examined closely, they serve not only as a definition, but also set out the training application actions necessary before validation can be approached—"behavioral," "objectives," "realistically based," "initial identification of training needs," "criteria," "organization." Without the application of these activities, any subsequent validation ceases to have any value.

The definition of *evaluation* is:

The assessment of the total value of a training system, training courses, or program in social as well as financial terms. Evaluation differs from validation in that it attempts to measure the overall cost benefit of the course or program and not just the achievement of its laid down objectives. The term is also used in the general judgmental sense of the continuous monitoring of a program or of the training function as a whole.

Finally, the MSC defines *assessment* as:

A general term for the process of ascertaining whether training is efficient or effective in achieving prescribed objectives. It covers both validation and evaluation.

My simpler explanation of these definitions is that *evaluation* covers training and its real benefits at work from beginning to end, whereas *validation* concentrates on the effectiveness of the training in relation to the training alone. *Assessment* is the process of measuring both validation and evaluation.

WHAT WE WANT TO KNOW

Whatever words we use to describe what we are doing or what we should be doing and achieving, the aim is to ensure that our training is effective for both the learner and the organization. This means we need to ask certain questions and obtain meaningful answers; these questions include both *validation* and *evaluation* as defined earlier:

1. Has the training satisfied its objectives?
2. Has the training satisfied the objectives/the learning needs of the clients?
3. Can it be demonstrated at the end of the training that these objectives have been met?
4. Are people operating differently at the end of, and as the result of, the training?
5. Did the training contribute directly to this different behavior?
6. Could the behavioral change have been obtained in a different way?
7. Is the learning achieved being used in the real work situation?
8. Has the training/learning contributed to the production of a more efficient and effective worker?
9. Has the training contributed to a more effective and efficient (hence more cost and value-effective) organization?

Validation Questions

More specific questions are raised that we might validate and evaluate the training provided.

Training content.   Is the material contained in the training program complete to the extent of the required criteria? Is it relevant to the skills, knowledge, or attitudes being presented? Is it up to date? Are there processes established to maintain these requirements?

Training methods.   Are the methods, techniques, and approaches the most appropriate ones for this subject, this level and status of learner, and so on? Were the methods used the most appropriate for the learning styles of the learners?

Learning amount. What material was included in the course? Was it new to the learner or, perhaps because prior knowledge had not been determined, repeated material? Despite being repeated material, did this repetition materially assist the learners to come to terms more effectively with the material?

Length and pace of the training. If the material included satisfied the content criteria, was the event of an effective length and pace? Were all aspects afforded their required time and emphasis? Were some areas overemphasized and others underemphasized?

Objectives. Did the training event satisfy its stated behavioral objectives? Were the learners given any opportunity to try to satisfy their personal objectives? Was this opportunity accepted? Were personal objectives actually satisfied?

Omissions. Were any essential aspects omitted from the learning event? Did time constraints, excess material, or incorrect approaches contribute to these omissions?

Transfer to work. How much of the learning is likely to be transferred to work on the learner's return there? What factors will encourage or inhibit this transfer? To what extent will the learner's manager be involved in this transfer?

Relevance. Was the course/seminar/workshop/conference/tutorial/coaching assignment/project/open learning system the most appropriate means of approaching these learning needs? Would more or as much learning have been achieved by some other application? Would as much learning have been achieved without any training intervention?

Environment. Was the training environment the most appropriate for the learning—hotel, conference center, organization training establishment, space at the work establishment (training room), at the person's workplace? Were the environmental conditions conducive to learning—comfort, heating, noise, visibility? Were the arrangements satisfactory—food, sleeping accommodation, study accommodation?

Finally, and very relevant to the overall subject of this book:

The trainer. Did the trainer have the necessary skills, knowledge, attitudes, techniques, approaches, and methods to present the material in such a way that learning was encouraged?

Evaluation Questions

Questions need to be asked following the validated training events to ensure the training/learning is put into operation for the benefit of the learner and the organization. Examples of questions of evaluation are:

Application of learning. Which parts of the individual's work now include elements that are a direct result of the training event? Which new aspects have already been introduced as a result of the learning? Which parts of the previous work have now been replaced or modified as a result of the training and learning? Which relevant and accepted elements of the training have not yet been applied? Why not?

Efficiency and effectiveness. How much more efficient and/or effective is the level of work now being achieved? Is this the result of the training? If not, how has it been achieved?

Training hindsight. With the passage of time and attempts to apply the learning, are there any amendments to the end-of-training validation responses that were given?

The questions relating to the validation of the training are normally posed either at the end of the training program or soon after its conclusion, and the valuation questions at a later stage. At this later stage, some 3, 6, or 12 months after the end of the training, the questions can be asked of both the learner and the learner's supervisor, both of whom should state their own viewpoints. As we discussed earlier, the line supervisor must be interested in this process for the training to have any effectiveness.

THE VALIDATION TRAIL

Validation should not be confined to the end of the training event, although it is common for the trainer, training manager, or senior management to ask for validation:

- Immediately after the start of the training course.
- During the progress of the training course.
- At the end of the training event.
- Sometime after the actual end of the event.

Under such circumstances, validation has no value. The basic requirement of any form of validation or evaluation is to have some measure of the learner's starting point before the training. If the learner's level of knowledge, skill, or attitude is not known before the training starts, it will be impossible to assess whether there has been any improvement. Improvement over what? Often, at the end of a training event, it is said: "Oh, yes. They have all improved considerably." This statement has no value.

Before we can start looking at any measures for validating the training event, it is necessary to consider what can and must be done before the training.

TRAINING ANALYSES

The training trail begins with training needs identification. Needs are often expressed without any real analytical approach: "It would be a good thing if such and such a training course was put on!" I am assuming here that someone in an organization has determined that training in certain aspects is necessary for the well-being of the organization's individuals and the organization itself. An analysis of this nature is obtained from such events as:

- The introduction of new work.
- The injection into the organization of a number of inexperienced workers.
- Direct observation that certain aspects of work are not being performed effectively.
- Indirect evidence (for example, a reduced number of sales or production of items or continuance of clients) that certain areas of the work are not being performed effectively.
- A request by individuals or groups of individuals for training in certain subjects for whatever reason.

- The completion of annual job appraisal reports that show training need.
- The introduction of a development program.

Many of these pieces of evidence that training is required are little more than an indication, and it is necessary for a more detailed analysis to be performed. This book is not the place for a full description of these essential activities, but the next requirement is usually the production of a specific job description linked with a person specification. The matching or nonmatching of these two factors determines the skill gaps and hence the training specification.

This approach is particularly relevant in the analysis situations shown above where

- New work is being introduced.
- Inexperienced workers are being recruited.
- Work is not being performed effectively.
- Development is seen as necessary.

Job Analysis, Description, and Specification

The job description.   The job description is the first level of the final job specification or task analysis and describes the job, at the responsibility level, in a fairly general way. In some analyses, these are known as key purposes or units of work or, in management by objectives approaches, as key result areas or tasks. The job description gives the principal areas of work and responsibility and such aspects of the job as lines of responsibility and communication and hours of work. A typical job description for a hotel receptionist is shown in Figure 6–1.

The job description in Figure 6–1 is too broadly described to be useful in identifying training needs and presents only the baseline for the full description of a job, its duty requirements, and responsibilities. It does supply an outline and starting point from which more detailed requirements can be identified.

The job specification.   The job specification enlarges on the job description, and it is here that the areas of possible training needs are found. In the specification, each general area of responsibility or unit of work is examined to produce a detailed requirement of the job. The

FIGURE 6–1
Example of a Job Description

Job Title:	Hotel Receptionist
Function:	To maintain the hotel's bookings, reservations, and charge system, and be the hotel's principal customer contact point.
Lines of Communication:	Upwards—to Head Receptionist Laterally—to other Receptionists Downwards—to Junior Receptionists and Hall staff
Responsibilities	To—Head Receptionist For—Junior Receptionists
Hours of work:	Shift system (detailed according to practice)
Duties:	1. Dealing with room reservations made by telephone, letter, fax, and customer contact. 2. Allocating reservations and completing records of these reservations. 3. Confirming reservations with customers by the appropriate means.

specification offers in detail what the jobholder should be able to know and do and identifies the attitudes and manner needed to perform the job effectively.

An example of a straightforward job specification, or at least part of it, is shown in Figure 6–2. A painter and decorator has a number of units of work, one of which is paperhanging. Part of the job specification for the paperhanging element of the painter and decorator's work is shown.

In this example, only some of the elements of one unit of work have been given, divided into knowledge and skills. Other elements are concerned with the preparation for paperhanging, the actual paperhanging, and the post-task operations.

The more detailed and complete the job specification, or task analysis, the more likely it is that the training needs analysis will be sufficiently accurate and comprehensive. This analysis is the first line of attack in producing terminal training objectives for the training event, the measures by which the effectiveness of the training can be assessed.

Training Objectives

The difference between the identified, detailed needs of the job in terms of knowledge, skills, and attitudes and the knowledge, skills, and attitudes of the jobholder or potential jobholder determine the training

FIGURE 6–2
Example of Part of a Job Specification

Job title: Painter and decorator
Duties: 3.   Paperhanging
                        3.1   Task: Selection of paper
                              Knowledge: Types of wallcovering, including the
                                 strengths, textures, etc. of the materials
                              Skills: Ability to assess covering quantity by manual
                                 manipulation
                        3.2   Task: Measuring room
                              Knowledge: Methods of estimation, unit methods of
                                 measurement
                              Skills: Measuring in various unit methods.

---

needs, the so-called training gap. Once it has been decided that training should be given to fill this gap, the trainers can start designing a training event to satisfy these needs. The terminal training objectives should be considered first. These objectives describe in as much detail as possible, what, at the end of the training event, the learners will know, be able to do, and what their attitudinal behaviors will be—the training needs from the job and person specification described as end results. If, at the end of the training, the learners with these particular needs can show they have satisfied the training objectives and hence have satisfied their training needs, the training can be assessed as successful.

The training event is designed with these terminal training objectives in mind, taking account of all the factors we have already considered to ensure learning is achieved in the most effective way.

The next step, in association with pre-training measures, is to design the end-of-training validation instruments. An important part of that statement, and one that is often ignored, relates to the pre-training measures. Again, we return to the truism, "If you don't know where you have come from, how will you know how far you have come and whether the end of the journey has been achieved?"

In most cases, training events have been designed for groups of individuals with common learning needs. Within these groups, virtually every individual has a different need and different levels of knowledge, skills, and attitude. Consequently, the training must be designed not only to satisfy the overall terminal objectives, but also to cope with the individual needs.

Because the training needs to fill gaps in the skill levels of individuals who will participate in the training, it is essential to analyze the potential pool of learners.

In the case of training that focuses on new needs for an existing work force, it is far easier to develop a profile of the trainees. This profile should focus on the current skill level of both the individual and the collective group. Existing personnel records and prior training allow the training manager or designer to access a large body of critical knowledge about the level of the group, which types of training events have worked best in the past with the group, and so on.

When the training is for people not currently employed by the corporation, it becomes a little more difficult. In this case, a profile of the anticipated skill needs can be developed, often aided by the use of résumé material of candidates for the positions not yet hired.

It is important at this stage, when the initial design is being created, that the training department work closely with the supervisors who will have responsibility for the new workers. In some cases, a combined profile can be created through the use of résumé material of potential employees and a mock-up of the skills the direct supervisors believe will be most important.

Because the training must address both the trainees and the subject matter if it is to be successful in transferring knowledge into job action, this step is crucial.

Training Design

Once the job specification has been firmly established and the basic training needs of the population identified as accurately as possible, the training staff can design an appropriate training program. This should reflect:

- The training needs identified from the task and person analyses broken down into manageable learning blocks.
- The training content relevant to the needs of the individual and the organization.
- The course/workshop/seminar/sessions/learning package pitched at the appropriate level.
- The specific terminal objectives that are, as far as possible, quantifiable, active, measurable, and time bounded.
- The learning preferences of the learners taken into account as far as they are known and as far as the training will allow.

- Learner involvement to the optimum extent.
- The insertions of appropriate tests/validations at the relevant times.
- Selection of the most appropriate and effective trainers for the event.
- Selection of the most appropriate environment available for the event.

These requirements should be met by whoever is to be responsible for the training validation (and subsequently the trainer assessment) for an assessment of the competence level of the training and its design. The planning and design factors, as we saw earlier, are highly indicative of the skills of an effective trainer and as such feature strongly in any assessment of the training and the trainer.

It is difficult for any potential assessor, other than in self-assessment, to have direct access to the planning and design activities of the trainer and consequently to have a full knowledge of all the elements that have led to the design of the training. The effective trainer should have satisfactory documentation to show and support the steps taken in job and task analysis, needs analysis and plans for implementation leading to the training design, plans for the presentation of the training (including notes on techniques methods, approaches, activities), and details of the validation actions. Without these, the assessor—whether the training manager or the trainers themselves—cannot ensure valid assessment of the training.

Chapter Seven

Training Validation at Work

The previous chapter considered the value of assessing the training event as part of the assessment of the trainer. Perhaps this area of assessment in training has distracted attention from measures to assess the trainer. Although approaches to training validation are many and varied, it is surprising how many organizations involved in training give little priority, if any, to training validation.

In any consideration of the effectiveness of a trainer or group of trainers, the effectiveness of the training itself must be a powerful measure in addition to direct assessment of the trainers. Training validation is one of the more objective measures the trainers can utilize in self-assessment. Some assessors assert the training validation is all that is necessary, because if the measures show the training is valid, the trainers must be effective. This is a strong argument, but requires much supportive evidence.

Assessment of the trainer also gives additional information about whether there are any particular strengths or weaknesses that can be improved or utilized more effectively in other situations. Although the course validations show effectiveness, this may or may not be due to the trainer—there are intelligent trainees! And if the trainer, who may not be completely effective, is helped to improve, the training may become even better and an easier learning event for the trainees.

These are but a few of the reasons both approaches are necessary. Assessment can be made using either, but there are benefits in using both.

TRAINING INVENTORIES

Assessment instruments are required for assessing knowledge, skills, and/or attitudes at various stages of training. Some aspects of training are not sufficiently sensitive to measurement to permit completely objective assessment. Many of these are the human relations type of training. Such training areas as people skills, interpersonal and interactive skills, and even the more apparently objective types of people training such as leadership, supervision, presentation, and so on have varying degrees of objectivity and consequently affect the assessment.

Some assessors even suggest that some forms of training—for example, management training—cannot be measured by validation. I cannot agree, although I accept that some aspects of training are highly subjective, in which case it is necessary to use more subjective forms of assessment, accepting their subjectivity and making allowances. Is it not better to attempt something than to do nothing at all, however imperfect that something might be?

Assessment of the effectiveness of such training as interpersonal skills is particularly difficult. Assessment might be made by an external observer—What are the standards of interpersonal effectiveness to which that individual works? Are they the same as others'? Are they in line with an "accepted" model? Can an individual assess his own effectiveness, as we so often ask? Again, what standards are used in this self-assessment?

Assessments can be made, even in these difficult areas. For example, the external observer may use behavior analysis, an accurate form of behavior observation and recording, but one that requires a subjective model of behavior from which to work. If self-assessment is required, the classical pre- and post-tests fall down for a variety of reasons. Modification of this, such as the Three-test, can be introduced, which reduces some of the inherent subjectivity.

When technical, procedural, systems types of training are considered, assessment of the effectiveness of the training is relatively simple. For example, the objective of a training course for newly appointed gas meter readers might be expressed as: "By the end of the training, each person will be able to read 100 meters of the clock variety to an accuracy of 95% during a period of x minutes." Two tests would be necessary for this training. Before the training started, it would be necessary to set a practical test of meter reading for the trainees—for example, 100 meters might be made available and the trainees given the instruction to read as many of them in x minutes as possible. The number of meters read during the period and the reading accuracy could then be measured. At the end of the training, the same test would be repeated (the classical pre- and post-test procedures) and if the objective stated above was fulfilled by all the trainees, the training would have been 100 percent effective. If this situation were repeated with a number of different instructors and the same results achieved, every indication would be that the training content, methods, and so on were the contributory factors to the success rather than the trainers.

Not all training is as straightforward as this, however. When we assess the more subjective training subjects mentioned earlier, it is often the skill of the trainer that produces the training result, rather than the training material.

PRE-TRAINING ASSESSMENT

The three principal stages of assessment covered here—pre-training, during training, and end of training—all reflect the three major aspects of training—knowledge, skills, and attitudes.

Knowledge

Unless the subject is specialized, trainees will have some knowledge of the subject before a training course. This is certainly true of the more mature learner, or those who are already employed in the company, industry, or industry sector. It may be less likely if new entrants to the job, company, or industry are involved. Learners should, therefore, be tested before training so the effectiveness of the training can be assessed. Both oral and written tests are available, although some form of written rather than oral test is both preferred and more common.

Open answer. Probably the most common form of test of knowledge phrases questions so there is no clue to the answer. Typical examples of this approach are:

Compare the advantages and disadvantages of. . . . Discuss the effects of "x" on subject "y" during period "z."

Two main problems are found with this type of test:

1. The question has to be put in such a way that it is completely understandable in exactly the same way by all the people being tested. There is little value if the question is seen to be asking different things by several different people.
2. The answers will be given, usually in open text, in the style and to the extent determined by the respondent. Consequently, if 20 people are asked to complete the question, the responses will

almost certainly be given in 20 different ways—construction, grammar, spelling, content. All of these need to be assessed and compared with a set standard.

If the test is repeated at the end of the training, the improvement in responses indicates the effectiveness of the training; they are less likely to reflect the effectiveness of the trainer.

Binary choice questions. Rather than asking for open answers, with the resulting difficulties summarized above, binary choice questions can be used. The simplest forms of these ask a question and offer a choice between two responses, usually either yes/no or short phrases. An example of this type of test is:

(Delete inappropriate answer)

1. Does your company offer annual appraisal interviews?

Yes/No

2. How effective does the company report state that these appraisals are?

Effective/Very Ineffective

3. Does the annual company report state whether these appraisals are wanted by the employees?

Yes/No

Such a technique is very limited, but the questions can follow a progressive line in relation to the training given. The benefits of this type of test are:

- The questions can be related to earlier stages of the training.
- The marking/scoring is much easier than assessing open answers.
- Consistent "correct" answers can be agreed on before the training.

Fairly specific rules must be followed or the test will lose some of its objectivity:

- Language must be chosen carefully to prevent ambiguous questions. This is not as easy as it sounds. Consider question 1 above; would everybody understand the word *offer* in exactly the same way, or would some people interpret it in a different way, and would some people have doubts as to what exactly was meant?
- The question posed must be singular; that is, it must consist of only one part to prevent confusion. The intention is to determine

the extent of the knowledge of the learners, not to test any other skills they may have.

• One of the answers given in the binary choice must be correct, and there must be no ambiguity or doubt about is correctness.

True/false questions. Like the binary choice approach, the true/false test offers a choice of two answers. For example,

(Put a line under the correct answer)
A red light signifies that the machine is in operation

True/False

This test must follow the same guidelines given for the binary choice test and has the similar advantage of simplicity of scoring, but it also suffers from the same disadvantage in that the learner may be tempted to guess the answers, having a 50-50 chance of being correct. The total response follows the laws of probability, although the test is intended to assess real knowledge.

Multiple choice questions. One way of avoiding the problem of guesswork contaminating the real knowledge level is to offer a number of choices. The number of choices usually ranges between three and five, although it can be readily extended to seven. A "silly" answer is often included in the list, although if the answer is too silly there seems to be little reason for its inclusion. A typical five-choice questions could be:

(Circle the number of the answer you think is the correct one)
The company's annual job appraisal review interview is
1. Mandatory for all staff.
2. Mandatory for all staff from supervisor level up.
3. Voluntary for all staff.
4. Voluntary for all staff up to the age of 60.
5. Voluntary for all staff over the age of 60.

The multiple choice test is more difficult to construct than the previous examples because of the need to produce a number of alternatives for each question, but scoring or marking is simple against a "correct" score sheet.

The example quoted above is one variation of this type of test—the incomplete answer test, because one of the alternatives offered completes the sentence correctly. An alternative approach is to offer alternative choices to the question. For example:

(Please circle the number of the statement you think is correct)
What are the recommended tire pressures for a 1992 Chevrolet Corvette?
1. 28 lb/in^2 front and rear
2. 30 lb/in^2 front and rear
3. 28 lb/in^2 front, 30 lb/in^2 rear
4. 30 lb/in^2 front, 28 lb/in^2 rear
5. 40 lb/in^2 front and rear

Open short answers. Another test is one in which an incomplete statement is given. To complete the statement, the learner has to supply a short answer. In some cases this might be one word or figure:

The minimum stopping distance for a car traveling at 40 mph in dry road conditions is. . . .

In other cases, the learner may have to give a short explanation in his own words. Although the answers may not be capable of being scored as quickly as the tests where a choice of answers is given, the responses are usually short enough to be scored quickly. This is a recommended form of testing because, like the open answer type of test, the responder has to know the answer and be capable of expressing it, but scoring the responses is not a problem. The responses to this type of test can demonstrate more than simple rote learning and consequently indicate training quality.

SKILLS

Skills are the practical outcomes of knowledge, understanding, and the ability to put them into practice, whether they are already held or have been acquired through training. Consequently, tests of skill are required in training whenever a trainee needs to be able to translate learning into practice. Such tests may include those to measure:

- The quality of a finished task.
- The accuracy of a physical or mental operation (this will link directly with the knowledge tests to determine whether the trainee can do what he knows).

- The speed of task completion where speed is part of the task requirement.
- Completeness in performing the task (there is little value in performing a task perfectly if the whole task is not complete).
- Abilities in planning, organizing, communicating, designing, and so on (these may have been part of the training at the theoretical, model level—can the trainee put the model into real action, or, if pretesting, does the potential trainee have any idea what he is trying to do?).
- Competence in correctly identifying mechanical components and completed written procedures.

Interpersonal skills are generally excluded from this list because they are much more subjective and much more difficult to measure.

Implementation of Skills Tests

Skills tests should be relatively easy to apply to trainees when they attend a training course or before attempting a learning package, provided either a specific end product or a qualified observer is present to validate the skill. Often trainees attend the training because it has already been assessed in the workplace that they are unable to fulfill the necessary skill standards. It would be unwise for the trainer to agree to accept a trainee in his course without testing whether the potential trainee has the skill to learn and the level of any skills he possesses.

Construction of Skills Tests

Although there is as much, if not more, variety in skills testing as there is in knowledge testing, test construction must follow a set of specific guidelines to ensure the tests are valid—to be able to do the task is not a sufficient test of competence and skill.

1. The skills test must be directly related to the final training objective. There is always a great temptation for trainers to set high skills standards to see whether the trainees can cope with more than is necessary. If the trainee proves this, so what? If every trainee shows he is capable of more than the terminal objective for this task, either the training population is the wrong one, the training task has been set at too low a level, or there is no need for the training and the training needs analysis has

been faulty. One expression often used in training is "Why give Rolls-Royce training when Compact training is all that is required!"

2. The test, and the terminal objective, must be completely accurate and accepted within the occupation and the organization. The terminal objective will have an end product, but other actions will precede it. This is similar for the test. In real work practice, experienced workers may cut corners to save time and energy. The terminal objective must ensure these shortcuts are not trained for—if the organization subsequently permits them, fine, but training must follow the recognized, safe, complete path. In the same way, the test must be designed and/or scored on the basis that a certain procedure has to be followed.

3. The instructions for the test, the skill level possible, the time available, and any other factors should be unambiguous and every effort should be made to ensure the potential trainees understand what they have to do. It is also valuable at the pre-training stage to let the testees know they are not necessarily expected to complete the test, and it is intended to determine their skill level.

4. The trainers must ensure, as far as possible, before the test is used that it is a valid test and will not need modifications for further use. If not, different groups will be unfairly tested with different instruments, however small the modification may be. The tests must be presented in exactly the same way on each occasion, irrespective of who is presenting them. It is valuable to have a written briefing, which itself has been validated, that can be either read by the testees or, preferably, read to them by the tester.

5. The test environment should replicate the conditions under which the skill is to be performed; often the best place is in the workplace. Situational realism is highly desirable when emergency skills are being considered, but modifications often have to be made or simulations introduced to avoid dangerous situations. This was the principal reason for the development of the flight simulator in the training of aircraft pilots.

6. The scoring, marking, or assessment system must be standardized so different testers will not assess in different ways. The test must avoid the dangers of accepting that the testee "was about to do that anyway."

7. The test, at least for the terminal objective testing, must have a realistic but challenging performance criterion. I have seen too many training objectives that require the trainee to show in the final test a competence level of 75 or 80 percent. Some tasks require 100 percent competence—would you be happy about flying with a pilot who had

achieved 85 percent competency? What if the remaining 15 percent competence was needed on an occasion when he was flying the aircraft on which you were a passenger? Or the welder who is required to achieve a 90 percent competence level. If the object you were using had been welded and failed because of that 10 percent, would you be in a position to complain? These are obviously life and death situations, but even if a task is not of this order, there is little justification in not aiming for 100 percent success at the end of the training program. Settling for less is accepting that the training is less than 100 percent itself.

Subjective Skills

It is much more difficult to design, apply, and score tests for the more subjective skills than for the mechanical, systems, and procedural task skills. In the latter, absolute standards can be applied so the results can be validated with a reasonable amount of accuracy. When we talk about other kinds of skills, however, many more difficulties of assessment appear.

Take, for example, an intended course of training for managers in negotiating skills. The pre-tests could take various forms. The manager's manager might state that his subordinate "needs to be better at negotiating." Attempts to elucidate this statement in quantitative terms are often doomed. The question can be asked, "Why do you say he needs to be better?" The responses can range from the almost impossibly subjective, "Oh, I just think he does," to an apparently objective statement that he "failed" in his last six negotiations. Behind this latter statement, there may be many more reasons than lack of skill, although that may be the prime consideration. It may be that the last six negotiations were impossible ones in which to succeed; a number of backup conditions did not support his negotiating; the power base in the negotiation gave him no chance of succeeding; and so on.

In testing subjective skills, there are usually indications of a training need that have to be investigated in as many ways as possible.

Pre-testing Subjective Skills

The first requirement has to be acceptance by the tester that the methods of assessing subjective skills will almost certainly be subjective and the results will be open to challenge. This being accepted, it is usually necessary to approach the pre-testing in a number of ways. The views of the individual's superior(s) must be considered as well as the views of the potential trainees—whether by interview response, self-assessment inventory, and/or track record.

Rarely does the tester have an opportunity to observe the individual actually in the situation. The next best trial situation is at the start of the course with a simulation. In the skill area we are discussing, this would be a simulated negotiation, either with the training staff or with fellow course members, under the observation of the training staff.

Even these assessments must be necessarily subjective because any assessment has to be made against a model standard accepted by the trainer and the organization. Does the organization require win/lose or win/win negotiators? This will make a difference to the initial assessment, the training course, and the terminal objectives. How capable are:

1. The senior managers of making assessments of skill.
2. The potential trainee of making a self-assessment (and against which criteria).

In the case of the potential trainee, I have determined an approach (known as the Three-Test) that will be referred to later as reducing the subjectivity of self-assessment.

The most the trainer can hope for at this stage is an amalgamation of views that cumulatively will help to build a picture of the potential trainee's apparent skill. It is helpful if any tests given at this stage are repeated at the end of the training—they may not be accurate, but at least they are roughly comparable. The problem is that real-life assessors—the trainees' managers—may not have any better criteria against which to assess the individual once he has been trained. Assessment in these cases is very difficult, perhaps impossible, but I believe that attempting something is better than doing nothing.

ATTITUDE PRE-TESTING

If the approach to skills testing in some areas is difficult, attempting to do the same for attitudes is even more so. Attitudes and behavior are completely subjective, objectivity being approached only by models based on existing cultures. Even so, these cultures change over time, from country to country, from class level to class level, and from individual to individual. Any organization that involves itself in attitude training, and the borders between attitudes and skills are very hazy, must define exactly what attitudes and behavior it will treat as the norm of the organization.

This is made even more difficult when relationships, negotiations, and other forms of contact are increasingly being made between cultures. Business approaches between western and eastern cultures have to be tailored to these differences in values and attitudes. Consequently, when we are trying to assess the effectiveness of attitude training, the base model, however subjective, must be clear.

Apart from the subjective appraisal of individuals by their managers, most of the pre-tests for attitude aspects are based on self-assessment inventories. These are notoriously subjective and open to distortion, deliberate or unconscious. Again, assessments at this stage must be validated as far as possible by multiple assessments.

The observational technique known as behavior analysis, a very useful form of activity analysis, can be invaluable at this stage if:

- A qualified observer is available to use the analysis.
- Time is available to perform the analysis.

This technique will be described later.

Self-Assessment

The most common form of assessment for attitude rating is the use of some form of self-assessment inventory. If self-assessment is used in the simple, classical pre- and post-test approach, severe discrepancies can result, but these can be minimized by the three-test method (see page 111). The format of the self-assessment inventory depends on the area of attitude training being considered. If this is, for example, interpersonal skills, a typical questionnaire might be that shown in Figure 7–1.

The methods for assessing various types of training are many and varied. Although there is not necessarily one approach for each type of training, different tests are more effective with certain types of training. Each training event must be evaluated to determine the most appropriate and effective form of validation.

FIGURE 7-1
Behavior Self-Assessment Questionnaire

Ellray Associates
Behavior Skills Questionnaire

NAME _____ DATE _____

Please enter a check alongside each item on the scale 1 to 10 representing where you consider your present level of skill might be.

	LOW	HIGH
	1 2 3 4 5 6 7 8	9 10

1. Being aware of my own behavior
2. Being aware of the reaction of others to my behavior
3. Being aware of the behavior of others
4. Being aware of my reactions to the behavior of others
5. Being aware of how much I talk
6. Being aware of how much I support others
7. Being aware of how much I build on others' ideas
8. Sensing the feelings of others
9. Being aware of how much I interrupt others
10. Being aware of how much I really listen to others
11. Telling others what my feelings are
12. Being aware of what behavior modification I need to do
13. Knowing how to modify my behavior
14. Being aware of how much I bring out the views of others

1 2 3 4 5 6 7 8 9 10

Chapter Eight

Ongoing Assessment

The main purpose of validation is to determine the change in knowledge, skills, and/or attitudes as a result of the training. During training events lasting longer than three days, it is advisable to maintain an ongoing validation of the effectiveness of the training. Doing without it (and its occurrence is by no means universal, sometimes for valid time and resource reasons) can suggest:

- The trainer is not interested in the progress of his training (and therefore is not an effective trainer).
- The trainees and their needs are being ignored.
- The training may be proceeding in a completely ineffective way.

The interim validation need not be a major operation. It usually occupies only a short time each day, although some approaches are much more complex and require more time. It is crucial that

- The feedback given by the trainees is listened to by the trainers.
- Sufficient time is given to show that the operation is an important aspect of the training.
- The trainer has the authority to act on any feedback.

If all these criteria are not followed, interim validation has little value and any efforts will reveal the trainer to be ineffective.

SESSION AND DAILY VALIDATION

The simplest form of interim validation is a constant check on progress after each session or day during the training event. The approaches are virtually the same as the pre-training techniques for knowledge, skills, and attitudes.

In the case of knowledge training, tests can be applied at relevant intervals, the content based on the stage of learning that should have been achieved by that time. These tests should be of the same nature as the pre-training tests.

Skills training, whether of mechanical objective or subjective skills, can similarly produce interim validation tests and inventories, like those we discussed in the pre-training stage.

In the more general areas of skills training, usually some form of questionnaire is completed after a particular training session or at the end of a training day, in an attempt to check that the learners have progressed sufficiently along the determined training path.

As suggested this can be in the form of a practical test or, if this is not the type of training involved, a questionnaire based on the material that has been presented and should have been learned. The type of questionnaire will be considered later, but the timing of these approaches can be critical.

If the training is divided into specific sessions that are complete units in themselves, testing can be carried out with validity after each session. One danger is that learners might react against the overuse of tests and questionnaires, making them counterproductive.

Many general training events do not have strictly defined sessions. If the validation is completed immediately after the session, the principal advantage is that the learners will not have had any opportunity to forget whatever they learned from the session; neither will they have had the opportunity to reflect on the lessons presented, particularly if the learning preference of the individual is reflective and the training has perhaps been a complex activity.

The principal disadvantage is when the sessions are not unique or self-contained. Many courses use an input session, followed by an activity, followed by a discussion, followed perhaps by a video, then a final discussion, all on the same topic. The session alone may not have made much impact on the learners and perhaps they could not even see the importance or significance of their material. If a validation questionnaire is completed after the session in such circumstances, the comments would probably be far from favorable. At the end of the complete sequence, however, all the elements start to combine to make sense and the learners would have a better opportunity of realizing the value of the session. That would be the stage when completion of a validation instrument would have the most relevance.

Many training courses of several days' duration have a theme that runs for a complete day. In such cases, the end of the day is the most appropriate time to ask the learners to consider and report on the day's work. This can take several forms, usually either a verbal report or completion of individual reactionnaires.

If the feedback is to be verbal, care must be taken as to how this is approached. The most straightforward method is for the trainer to present the training group with a set of verbal or flip chart-presented questions about the learning, or even more simply to ask them what they have learned in the day's training. The report is taken immediately with the whole training group, in theory so everybody with anything to say can do so and be supported or contradicted by other members of the group. In practice, the comments are made by the strongest/most vocal/most articulate members of the group, and their views may not represent the views of the whole. My experience suggests that when there are one or two dominant contributors in the group, they usually want to demonstrate their "superiority" and challenge many aspects in an obstructive way.

One way to avoid bias is to give the group a set of questions about the day's training and ask the participants to write down their views. Once the views are written down, the open forum described above has a greater chance of hearing the opinions of the quieter members because they have something written on which to base their contributions—often a necessary aid for introverted people.

Many trainers divide the training group into smaller subgroups and ask them to produce a small-group view of the day's training and to appoint a reporter from each subgroup. At the report stage, the views of each group are given by the reporters, who need not necessarily agree with the views they are presenting. What is being presented are the views of the majority. There is always the chance the stronger members have dominated the subgroups, but if individuals have the opportunity to add anything after the reporter has made the group statement, the quieter members may be more likely to contribute if they disagree with the report because they have already spoken in the small groups.

LAST THING/FIRST THING?

Is it better to have the comments about a day's training immediately at the end of the day or the next morning? If the trainees are given overnight to reflect on the learning, with or without an aiding questionnaire, they will have had time to form an opinion. However, the opposite view holds that by the time the next morning comes, unless it is a very contentious issue, they may think the previous day is history and they want to get on with the new day's training. Whichever approach is adopted, the trainer must

- Allow sufficient time for discussion and comment.
- Be prepared to give time to clear any problems that may arise from the feedback.

It is often useful for an assessor of the trainer to sit in on these feedbacks, provided his presence is not seen as inhibiting. If the feedback reveals a number of points require clarification of some aspects of the training, this is very significant in an assessment of the trainer's skill. Such feedback must be taken as a pointer only, to be supported by other forms of assessment.

A PROGRESSIVE INTERIM VALIDATION

If the training has been particularly complex and the trainer wishes to assess the learning and is prepared to make a reasonable amount of time available, one approach is a useful extension of the simple feedback. This approach, which can occupy at least an hour, gives learners the opportunity to discuss the training event so far in as much detail as they wish, to compare their views with those of others, and to make decisions on the main areas on which they require some action. The end result of this method is sometimes simply that everything has been understood and is going well. There is no problem here because the trainer or assessor needs to know when things are going right as well as when they are going wrong. A complete endorsement is rare, particularly in difficult subject areas where there are no right and wrong answers. An example of this approach follows.

Say we have a group of 16 learners, not an unusual size for a training event. Ten is about the minimum size for this approach, but below this number it can still be applied with some modifications.

The training group is asked first as individuals to identify and write down for their own use three significant statements they would like to make about the event so far. This wording does not direct the learners to look at any specific aspect, good or bad, but gives them the opportunity to express a view on whatever they find important to them. Once the individual statements have been produced, the group is divided into eight pairs and asked to produce in each pair an agreed three significant statements from the six.

When the pairs have reached their conclusions, groups of four are formed—in this case, four groups. Six statements produced by the two pairs are brought to each group of four, and they are invited to refine these six into three statements.

At this stage, the groupings may vary. The four groups can be grouped into two sets of eight to produce two sets of three statements. Or the four groups can be brought into one group of 16 and asked to agree on 6 statements from the 12 they will bring with them. Whichever path is followed, the objective is to have six statements that have been discussed, argued over, negotiated, and agreed on.

The six statements, which will be of value in assessing the progress of the training, can then be listed on a flip chart with four columns to the right of the statements. The five columns can be headed "Strongly Disagree" (or SD), "Disagree" (or D), "Neither Agree nor Disagree" (or N), "Agree" (or A), and "Strongly Agree" (or SA), as demonstrated in Figure 8–1.

The learners are then invited to come to the flip chart and mark the column against each statement with their personal views. For example, a tick, cross, or asterisk could be used to enter these views in the relevant column—SA, A, N, D, SD. The resulting pattern will certainly indicate the significant views of the group and also show the number of those who are not with the majority. A discussion can then follow about the results, and the trainer must then take action to satisfy the stated needs of the learners.

OBJECTIVE OBSERVATION ASSESSMENT

In training events that are behaviorally anchored, the trainer can make an observational assessment of the progress and problems of the learners. If a number of activities during the training enable the learners to demonstrate their learning of the techniques, observation may be fairly simple. The actions and behaviors of the learners in these activities can be assessed against an accepted model of progress. Much of this assessment will be subjective. Even the model on which the observation is based may have highly subjective base values.

FIGURE 8–1
Interim Validation

Ellray Associates
During-Course Validation

Statement	SA	A	N	D	SD

BEHAVIOR ANALYSIS

Interaction analysis attempts to move away from the subjectivity of observation. Behavior analysis is a form of interaction analysis that is simple to operate and can be modified to suit a number of different types of learning events—interpersonal skills, interview training of various types, negotiation training, sales training, and so on. The variation for the event is introduced by changing the categories of observation.

The more usual use of behavior analysis (BA) is in the observation of verbal behaviors among individuals in groups and of the behavior of the groups themselves. The range of possible behaviors that can occur within any group is considerable, and the number of likely categories of behavior would make the analysis observation impossible. There are, however, a number of commonly occurring behaviors, and among these are a smaller number of behaviors that, if inappropriate, can be rectified by the person exhibiting them. Consequently, there is sense in observing behaviors that can be modified, rather than simply observing behaviors.

Neil Rackham, Peter Honey, and others were the initiators of this particular form of interactive analysis, and they produced a set of behavior categories, which are described in Figure 8–2.

Using a specially designed BA sheet with the categories entered and columns for the participants, the number of occurrences of each category of behavior against each participant can be logged and a pattern of behavior identified.

This approach is eminently suitable for certain occasions when a trainer is being observed for assessment. We shall return to this later.

FEELING REVIEWS

The final type of interim review to be described is related to assessing the feelings of the learners. Although it is directly aimed at encouraging feelings, the attitudes and views of the learners about the training, the trainer, and any other aspect can emerge.

There is a variety of ways of using this type of approach. My favorite way, particularly useful on interpersonal skill events, is to offer a "feelings review" at the start of each morning from the second day onward.

The individuals of the learning group are asked to think about and then write down three words or short phrases that express their feelings at that moment. No other directions are given on the basis that the main feelings that emerge will almost certainly be about the event. After obtaining the group's permission, the feelings of each learner are listed on a flip chart. Once all the words and phrases have been posted, the group is asked whether any member wishes to say anything about his choice of words or phrases or whether any other member wishes to ask the others about the words. The trainer will stop any discussion until all the entries have been made and then gently question some of the group about their choice of words.

The trainer, particularly on the second and subsequent uses of the approach, must be prepared for a serious, often lengthy, often emotional discussion in which he is often deeply involved. If certain feelings emerge in a number of learners, expressing doubt or hesitancy about something that has happened but will not be covered again, the trainer must take whatever action might be necessary to allay any fears or problems.

If a constant check is maintained by the trainer during a training event, and action is taken to remedy any deficiency discovered by any of the

FIGURE 8–2
Definitions of Behavior Analysis Categories

Proposing	Putting forward a new concept, suggestion, or proposal for positive action signaled by "I propose/suggest that . . . ," "I think we should . . . ," "Let's . . .". The more acceptable form of proposing may be to couch it in questioning terms (e.g., "What do you think about us doing . . . ?") rather than in the form of the statement. Proposals can come in a variety of forms that may need to be identified—procedure proposals, content proposals, accepted proposals, lost proposals.
Building	Extends or develops a proposal made by someone else, thus increasing its value, for example, "Let's go to the cinema" (proposal); "Yes. Let's go because there's a horror film on and we all like horror films" (building).
Seeking information, views, feelings, suggestions	A questioning behavior intended to obtain specific responses from another. (Questions can be phrased in a variety of ways—some effective, others generally not so effective.)
Seeking ideas	Specifically asking for proposals or suggestions to be made.
Giving information, views, feelings, opinions	Statements made by the contributors about their views, opinions, feelings, or giving information. Sometimes it can be difficult to differentiate between a statement and a proposal, particularly when the contribution is made in a confused or vague manner.
Disagreeing with reasons	A statement where the contributor disagrees with a proposal or statement made by another, but where the reasons for disagreement are stated fully.
Supporting	A conscious, direct, and positive declaration of support for a proposal or statement made by another.
Open	Usually an admission of guilt, or error, or inadequacy, made in a conciliatory rather than a defensive manner. Can be a simple statement—"I'm sorry."
Summarizing	A behavior particularly appropriate, though not exclusively, to a leader, where a full and accurate summary of what has transpired to that stage is given.
Attacking/defending	A behavior where one person, overtly, verbally, "attacks" another by the emotional use of words or tone of voice. "I might have expected you to say that" would probably be perceived as an attack on one's value judgments and would probably lead to a counterattack or the taking of a defensive stance.

FIGURE 8–2
(concluded)

Blocking	Contributions that add nothing to the discussion or place a block or difficulty in the path of the discussion and are usually bald statements. "Oh, we're just going around in circles" may be correct, but it does nothing to help the group forward. Facetious remarks, particularly when they become frequent, have the same effect.
Bringing in	A direct and conscious attempt to involve another person, usually inviting them by name. It is invariably linked with "seeking." In BA, two contributions are scored—one for the bringing in and the other for seeking.
Shutting out	An attempt, successful or otherwise, noticed or ignored, to exclude others. It can be by: interrupting another before they have finished speaking; side-talking when the rest of the group is discussing something; coming in when someone else has been invited to speak. As with "bringing in," two contributions should normally be scored—one for the interruption and the other for whatever contribution is made by the shutter-out (if this can be heard).

interim reviews, there is a greater likelihood that the training will be a success, not only because of the training content, but also because of the concern of the trainer.

A WORD OF CAUTION

In developing any interim review, it is important to remember the relationship between the length of the session each day and the length of the review. As each day's training progresses, the amount of time that can be spent in interim testing often increases because of the amount of material that has been covered. This can be very counterproductive to the interim review.

This is especially true for interim reviews that involve testing or questionnaires. The purpose of the interim review is to develop a sense of the efficiency of the training in reaching its goal of knowledge transfer, but the overuse of testing instruments can work to the detriment of the knowledge transfer process. The interim review should not overshadow the actual session work.

As discussed earlier, it is important to listen to the comments of the attendees. If those comments are focused on the testing measures rather than the course material, then the interim review process needs to be changed to reduce the focus on the interim review.

TRAINING VALIDATION INVENTORIES

The three stages of training validation—pre-, interim, and end-of-training assessments—are all equally important and should be made if the validation approach is to mean anything. However, for a variety of reasons—lack of resource, lack of time, disinterest, lack of knowledge and skill—frequently all these steps are not taken. Most often, some attempt is made at training validation at the end of the course. Even so, validation is rarely given the time and attention it deserves.

The principal purposes of end-of-course validation are to

1. Check whether the terminal objectives initially included in the course design have been fully or partially achieved.
2. Assess whether there has been any change in knowledge, skills, and/or attitudes of the learners (obviously if this hasn't been assessed before the training, end-of-course validation is a waste of time).

One factor in the equation of success or otherwise of the training is the role of the trainer. The validation of the training, as we saw earlier, will give very strong leads to this assessment.

KNOWLEDGE

The knowledge tests provided for the end-of-training validation are similar to those used in pre-training and interim validation. Preferably, the same tests should apply for the pre-test and for the post-test. The interim tests will be staged frequently, depending on the nature of the training.

The post-training tests must be applied scrupulously. They may reveal a wide range of gains in knowledge across the training group. It is too easy to accept the ones who do satisfactorily in the test as having benefited from the training, whereas the ones who do not do as well as having failed because of the type of people they are. If some learners do not perform in the test as well as the terminal objectives require, the following questions must be asked:

- Was the material the correct material?
- Was the training presented in the most appropriate way?
- Was the training provided in the most appropriate approach?
- Was the training material broken down into sufficiently digestible steps?
- Was the training material clear?
- Did the trainers check progress during the training?
- To what extent did the trainer present the training material in the most efficient and effective manner?

In using knowledge testing, or any of the various validity testing, to examine and assess the relative effectiveness of the trainer, it is important to understand that these tests can be manipulated in a number of ways by the trainer to skew the test results to benefit the assessment of the trainer.

This is true even on some standardized tests employed throughout the United States that feature multiple choice questions. If a multiple choice test does not penalize the person taking the test for a wrong answer, then the trainer can suggest before the test that all questions be answered regardless of whether the individual has even read the question. In this way, just on pure statistical probability, the final score for the individual will improve and a false measure of the trainer will be achieved. If there is a penalty for wrong answers or a balancing measure, then the trainer will focus the attention of the test taker to ensure the question is understood before answering. This is especially true in instances where there is no time limitation or where there is no penalty for completing only a portion of the test instrument.

As is discussed in other sections, when the measuring instrument is designed by the trainer, the ability to create a bias exists, and when this is coupled with the trainer's knowledge that the use of the testing results will be used in his evaluation, there exists a strong reason for leading the trainees into the evaluation instrument in a way that will produce better results.

Unfortunately, it is in those cases where a trainer is the weakest that this bias-directed testing may be most dominant. It is important that the person completing the evaluation analysis of the trainer be involved in developing the testing instrument or having the instrument developed by a professional or by someone other than the trainer.

SKILLS

Validating the learning of practical skills is generally as simple as testing of pre-training practical skills and knowledge as described above. Skill is the practical application of knowledge, thus demonstrating understanding. The potential gas meter reader who had no knowledge or skills in reading meters before the training can be checked by a practical test to see whether he has satisfied the prescribed terminal objectives. Can he read the number of gas meters required, to the required accuracy, within the prescribed time, exhibiting the appropriate attitudes? If so, the learner and the training have been successful. If not, the training has failed to achieve the objectives with that learner, and the questions listed above need to be asked.

SUBJECTIVE SKILLS AND ATTITUDES

When we try to assess whether the training objectives have been met, whether the learner has progressed, and whether the training has been validated, we meet the same problems we encountered with pre-testing. We are forced to rely on subjective assessments to reach any conclusions.

The use of questionnaires to answer subjective questions is widespread. The number of questionnaires or reactionnaires used by many trainers suggests we have attained a high level of skill and success with this approach. This is not the case, as is evident from the derogatory title of "happiness sheets" given to end-of-course questionnaires, many of which are designed to ensure a good rating is given for the training and the trainer. The questionnaire is completed in an obvious air of euphoria, and neither the trainer nor the learners give it the importance it deserves. It is in the interest of all trainers and all training managers or others who are responsible for assessing the effectiveness of training and the competence of trainers to ensure the end-of-course validation measures are effective and will reveal any existing problems. The most ineffective trainers are those who either continue training without modification even

though they know training is not achieving its objectives or are not aware
of whether the training is effective.

The variety of end-of-course validation instruments is extremely wide,
and there is room here to describe only one or two. Three important factors when asking learners to complete an end-of-course questionnaire or
other inventory are:

1. Allocating sufficient time for the learners to reflect on the training they have received, decide what they wish to say about it,
   and comment to a greater extent than simply marking a box on
   a checklist.

2. Constructing the questionnaire in such a way that any undue bias
   is avoided.

3. Emphasizing the importance of the assessments (to the training
   event, to the trainer, to the trainees because the assessment will
   be used within the continuing evaluation, and to future learners
   who will be attending the program). Trainees should also be told
   about what will happen to the completed inventories, who will
   see them, and how they will be used.

There is some argument as to whether the terminal validation questionnaire should be completed at the end of the course or when the
learner is back at work. If the questionnaire is completed at the end of
the course

- It may be completed in an atmosphere of euphoria or frustration,
  depending on factors that may have had nothing to do with the
  learning.

- Learners, because they are ready to leave the event, may not be
  able to give sufficient attention to reflect on what has happened
  and to assess the significant points.

I have found that both these arguments cancel each other out when the
points described above are followed. Once the validation is seen as part
of the event, the learners are more likely to give it the attention they gave
the rest of the training. The apparent advantages are:

- The training is fresh in the mind of the learners.

- Completion before the learners leave the training environment
  ensures 100 percent receipt of the assessments.

The benefits quoted for delaying completion until the learner has returned to work include:

- The opportunity for learners to translate their training/learning into the real work situation.
- Realistic completion of the inventory away from the atmosphere of the training event.
- The opportunity to reflect on the learning, its impact, its recall, and its validity.

These are strong arguments, but can be acceptable for validation purposes only if the questionnaires are returned for analysis. Those that are not returned may be the most important ones. Unless the organization has a system for ensuring the return of the questionnaires, there is a great danger that much less than 100 percent response will result. Many trainers consider a response rate of 33 to 50 percent as very good.

A low response rate is one of the problems of this approach. Another problem is that when the learners return to work, they become so immersed in catching up that the validation inventory loses any priority it may have had. Managers of learners are often to blame for this by not showing interest in the training event through a debriefing interview and failing to ensure post-training requirements are met.

The compromise is that the learners are asked to complete a questionnaire before they leave the training event (always bearing in mind the effectiveness criteria). A week or so after the event, the learners are sent the same questionnaire and asked to complete it and return it, considering the reflection they will have had since the end of the training. Some organizations require this follow-up questionnaire to be sent through the learner's supervisor, thus ensuring a much greater likelihood of completion and return.

CONSTRUCTING QUESTIONNAIRES

A large number of rules exist on the construction of valid questionnaires, based on sound psychological principles. Unless it is possible to assign the construction of a questionnaire to an expert in this field, it is most unlikely that the questionnaire used will satisfy all these requirements. One or two simple guidelines, however, will help the nonspecialist questionnaire constructor produce a suitable format.

The first question to ask is "What do I want to know?" followed very quickly by "What do I need to know?" It is easy to be persuaded to include questions that would be nice to know. The criterion must be "Do I need to know?" The questions you ask must

1. Differ from each other.
2. Be ones the learners will be able to answer.

In the first case, if the question is constructed in such a way that it is clear and satisfies the second point, there is no need to repeat the question in different words, as so often happens, "to ensure that I get the correct answers." Make the single question unambiguous and clear and you should receive all the information you require.

One factor to remember at all times is that the shorter the questionnaire, the better the response, especially if the questionnaire is to be completed after the event. Brevity does not obviate the need for completeness, and in some situations, the list of questions can be extensive.

Since the learners must be able to answer them,

1. The questions must relate to material that has been included in the training program (it is not the intention of the questionnaire to test the total range of the learner's knowledge).
2. The questions must be couched in language that will be understood without difficulty by the learners, even if this means using, say, three words instead of one.

The questionnaire must start with clear, concise, and unambiguous instructions. It is not sufficient to request that the respondents "indicate" which response they prefer, if there is no instruction about how to indicate—a cross, asterisk, circle, or any other defined mark.

The order of the questions can influence the types of responses. The rule is to start with general questions and move to more specific ones, in exactly the same way you would progress if you were conducting an interview. There may be some value in posing the most important questions early in the questionnaire because there may be a better chance of these being answered fully, particularly in a long questionnaire.

Closed questions should be avoided as much as possible, giving priority to more open questions, again as you would tend to do in an interview. If you ask a closed question, you may receive only a very limited answer and this requires you to ask yet another question, thus increasing the length of the questionnaire. An open question gives the opportunity of a more extended answer, but it does not guarantee you will receive a full answer.

Like the instructions, the questions must be clear, concise, and unambiguous. Some words add ambiguity and should be avoided because they often mean different things to different people, such as *often, frequently, extensively, most*. The questionnaire should use positive rather than negative questions, although again there are occasions when this is the only form of question possible. Ask only one thing in each question; if a question consists of multiple parts, the respondent can be confused about how to answer, particularly if the parts contradict each other. For example, the question "Do you enjoy driving, and if so, which is your favorite car?" contains two separate questions. If I had to answer that question, my answer to the first part would have no relationship at all to my answer to the second part. This is an obvious case for two separate questions.

Leading questions must be avoided, otherwise the respondent might think you are attempting to manipulate responses. Rather than ask "Don't you feel that the appraisal should be given every six months?" the format is more appropriate as "How often do you feel the appraisal should be made?" or even "How often do you feel the appraisal should be made? every month/every three months/every six months/annually? (circle the interval your prefer)." The latter might be used when brevity of response is required, although it has the disadvantage of suggesting you are leading the response to one of the alternatives given. Of course, this is exactly what you are doing, but this is justifiable if these are the only alternatives.

Finally, use of personal pronouns. Use at all times the relevant personal pronoun or personal possessive adjective—you, your, yours, my—rather than *one, one's,* and so on. This tells the respondent it is his views being sought.

If there is one central message in assessment, whether for training or the trainer, that message is continuity. Isolated assessments do little more than provide some information and certainly offer an incomplete, and sometimes erroneous, assessment. Continuous assessment demonstrates the progressive nature of training and the skill of the trainer at the various stages. Interim validation must be introduced only if there is the opportunity to take practical account of what emerges, particularly if it reveals the learners have not understood or accepted what has happened up to that stage. If there is no opportunity or intention to act as a result of the learners' comments, interim validation can be unnecessary.

Chapter Nine

End-of-Course Questionnaires

A wide range of questionnaires exists, varying from those that give a maximum amount of valuable information to those that give information in a misleading way. The following questionnaires are a brief selection only. Most of them can be modified if needed. Each gives you some information about the validity of the training and also, sometimes by inference and sometimes directly, the effectiveness of the trainer.

THE OPEN QUESTIONNAIRE

The open questionnaire is probably the simplest form of end-of-course validation questionnaire, and can be the most valuable because it gives the learners the complete opportunity to say whatever they wish about the training and associated matters. It consists of a blank sheet of paper on which the learners are invited to comment on whatever they wish (see Figure 9–1).

The advantages of this type of questionnaire are:

- It requires no construction of questions and so avoids directing or misdirecting the learners.
- Responsibility for the comments and which comments are made is passed to the learner.
- The format allows the learners to make comments on any matter they care to raise.

Disadvantages include:

- Comments may be made on subjects not related to the training (if desired, this can be avoided by asking the respondents to make

FIGURE 9–1
The Open Questionnaire

Ellray Associates
Measuring the Results

Please make any comments you feel are important or significant on any aspect of the seminar. You may wish to add your name.

---

their comments only on matters relating to the training; however, some valuable information might be lost if this injunction is made).

- Comments may not be made on the aspects of the most interest to the trainer. The omission of certain comments, which may have been anticipated by the trainer, may be highly significant. The trainer may have believed these omitted aspects were very important parts of the training content; the learners obviously did not think so. Alternatively, the trainer may have thought his presentation of certain parts of the training was exceptionally good, although the learners again clearly did not agree.

- It is very difficult to correlate the views of a number of learners because many of them will comment on exclusive and different subjects.

Because of these disadvantages, this form of reactionnaire, although very good for assessing training, is less useful for assessing the trainer (other than indirectly through the training assessment) because it does not address specific questions that will identify trainer skills.

FIGURE 9–2
The Open-Question Questionnaire

Ellray Associates
Measuring the Results

---

1. Which parts of the event did you find the most useful?
2. Which parts of the event did you find the least useful?
3. Are there any parts of the event you would omit? If so, which parts?
4. Is there anything you would wish to see added to the event? If so, what?
5. Which of your personal objectives were satisfied?
6. Which of your personal objectives were not satisfied?
7. Which aspects are you most likely to implement?
8. Any other comments?

Please add your name if you wish to do so.

THE OPEN-QUESTION QUESTIONNAIRE

The next step forward from the empty sheet is the open-question questionnaire, which directs the learners to certain areas, albeit fairly general, of the training program. Figure 9–2 shows a typical example.

The questions included on the form can be varied depending on the type of program, the information specifically required by the trainer, and so on. The main requirement is that the form ask open questions that will allow the learner to answer in any way he wishes and at any length. This is both an advantage and a disadvantage. Although the format is more directive than the previous questionnaire, the response—its content, extent, approach—is still in the hands of the learner. While this gives the learner a free hand in his answers and avoids any suspicion of manipulation, the nature of the responses can be so wide and varied that correlation is very difficult. In Figure 9–2, the questionnaire is principally directed at the effectiveness of the training and the actions resulting from it, but, if desired, an additional question or questions can be included directed specifically at the learners' reaction to the trainer. A question of this nature could be:

To what extent did the trainer contribute to any learning you have achieved?

How was that managed?

FIGURE 9–3
A Thurston Scale Questionnaire

A Manager's Responsibilities

(Circle either "A" or "D" for each statement)

1. A manager's first responsibility is the care of his staff.   A   D
2. A manager's first responsibility is to his employer.   A   D
3. A manager's first responsibility is to the objectives of the organization.   A   D
4. A manager must be able to do all the jobs of his staff.   A   D
5. A manager must know more than his staff.   A   D
6. A manager is closer to his staff than he is to his own line manager.   A   D

SEMANTIC DIFFERENTIAL AND SCORING QUESTIONNAIRES

In this type of questionnaire, scoring is possible, which presents the problem of possible overreliance on the scoring by the analyst. Because numbers are generally used in this scoring, the result tends to look mathematical, with all the logic and discipline this implies. Unfortunately, any scoring is highly subjective and must be treated as an indication only.

Three variations of the end-of-course validation questionnaire are commonly used.

The Thurston Scale

Numerical, quasi-mathematical scoring scales are not needed here because the method is similar to the binary method of knowledge testing discussed earlier.

The questions set are based on the whole course content (Figure 9–3). This scale gives the respondent the choice between agreeing or disagreeing with the statements made. There will always be cases where the choice is not black and white, which may give the learner the greatest difficulty in answering either A or D. To avoid this problem, when the questionnaire is issued, comments must be made that "A" = Agree, or agree more than you disagree; "D" = Disagree, or disagree more than you agree.

FIGURE 9–4
A Likert Scale Questionnaire

SA = Strongly agree
A = Agree
U = Uncertain
D = Disagree
SD = Strongly disagree

1. A manager's first responsibility is the care of his staff.   SA   A   U   D   SD
2. A manager's first responsibility is to his employer.   SA   A   U   D   SD
3. A manager's first responsibility is to the objectives of
   the organization.   SA   A   U   D   SD
4. A manager must be able to do all the jobs of his staff.   SA   A   U   D   SD
5. A manager must know more than his staff.   SA   A   U   D   SD
6. A manager is closer to his staff than he is to his own
   line manager.   SA   A   U   D   SD

The Likert Scale

The Likert scale overcomes the limitations of the Thurston scale by offering a wider range of options—the equivalent of the knowledge multiple choice test. Commonly five choices are given, although there is often argument about the middle choice, which offers uncertainty or neutrality. Figure 9–4 uses the same statements as Figure 9–3, but with additional choices.

Semantic Differential Scale

The most common scale in use is the one that uses a semantic differential at the poles on the scoring scale, with a range of score divisions between. For example, at one pole of the scale is the rating "good" and at the opposite pole the rating "bad". In questionnaires using this type of scale, the learners are asked to rate various factors on the scale. A typical example of this is shown in Figure 9–5, the event being part of the learners' assessment of a session on a negotiation skills course.

The individual respondents are required to rate the sessions using the scale divisions, usually a minimum of three, although five, six, or seven divisions are common. The respondents are asked to place a mark (tick, cross, asterisk, etc.) in the relevant division to which a number has been allotted.

FIGURE 9–5
Semantic Differential Scale Questionnaire

	6	5	4	3	2	1	
Learned a lot			X				Learned little
Enjoyed the session		X					Didn't enjoy the session
Understood everything		X					Understood nothing
Techniques were acceptable	X						Techniques were not acceptable

Session Negotiation Techniques

A useful numerical scoring basis for analysis is thus obtained, and a set of questions and scales can be used for each session, or any other item about which views are required.

There is often argument over the number of divisions on the scale. If there is an odd number of divisions, say seven, there will obviously be a middle division at four. The option to make such a score tends to be treated as the easy way out, either giving an "average" marking or marking that position if no decision can be made; both are "safe" markings. If this attitude can be overcome, the division "4" can be treated simply as what it is, a scoring position between 3 and 5. This attitude is possible but difficult to instill, owing to the widespread concept of middle position as average.

If only six positions are available for scoring, the respondents are forced to be positive in their assessments, putting their scoring either on the satisfactory or unsatisfactory halves of the scale.

Consistency is essential in the scoring numbering and in which extreme pole the "good" aspect is placed. It does not matter much whether the 6 or the 1 is on the left or right sides of the scale, whether "good" is on the left and "bad" on the right, or whether 6 is "good" and 1 is "bad." But the entries must be consistent throughout the questionnaire to avoid confusion. The more common custom, although not always adhered to, is to have the "good" or positive comment on the left side of the scale, linked with the higher number (e.g., good = 6, bad = 1).

One of the problems with the semantic differential scale is that the use of numbers gives the scale mathematical credence, while it is almost as subjective as "yes, no, don't know, might be, might not be." The scale has to be anchored with the polarized statements, which may be subjective, say:

"Completely . . . Not at all"

"To a very large extent . . . Hardly at all"

"To a maximum extent . . . To a minimum extent"

In practice, this may not present a problem because the divisions at the extremes are rarely used. This argues for the use of a scale with a greater number of divisions.

END-OF-COURSE ASSESSMENTS

Problems may arise in the scoring of semantic differential scales. The use of scores enables the numerical comparison to be made between course members and consecutive sessions or courses, but the number can become all-important to the trainer, who may evolve complex analytical assessments of the questionnaires. It can also be too easy for the learners simply to allocate scores, whether or not they have given sufficient consideration to the ratings.

A typical example of part of an end-of-course validation questionnaire is shown in Figure 9–6. The complete questionnaire can give what appears to be a picture of the success of the training, but this cannot be confirmed in any way other than by accepting the subjective, arbitrary allocation of scores.

If time for the validation measures is limited, and this is usually the case, the approach can indicate success of the training, and hence indirectly the effectiveness of the trainer.

While these differential scales are not accurate, they can be extremely valuable in certain instances for both trainer assessment and course content assessment. These instances center around when the choices of the trainees or learners are all in the most extreme pole positions or the division immediately next to the pole.

Most people completing a differential scale will avoid the "pole" positions in marking their choices except when they feel very strongly about their feelings, either positively or negatively. Thus, when the attendees cluster their marks around one of the pole positions on a specific item, this must be given even greater weight than normal. While the marking

FIGURE 9–6
An End-of-Course Questionnaire

Ellray Associates
Measuring the Results

Place a mark − X, *, 0), etc., in the division for which you wish to give the score.

A. Session: The skills of the effective trainer

		7	6	5	4	3	2	1	
Enjoyment	A lot								Little
Usefulness	A lot								Little
Content of session	Good								Poor
Extent of learning	A lot								Little

is subjective, there are generally at least one or two questions about which there will be a uniform marking clustered around one extreme or the other. This is critical to evaluation of both the content and the trainer since it is one of the few mathematically significant items that can be found on a scale of this nature. It is only mathematically significant in that it is a magnification of feelings from the remainder of the items being asked about in the questionnaire.

MORE DEMANDING VALIDATION

To try to avoid the problems of questionnaires giving a false impression ("happiness sheets", see page 97), some questionnaire designers add under the scoring scales a spaced headed "Comments." In my experience, such comments are either rarely made or have little value. A better way is to use a questionnaire designed particularly to elicit worthwhile comments. An example of this is shown in Figure 9–7.

In this example, the scoring scales are retained, but there is space to add questions other than those relating to learning. However, the questionnaire designer must be very clear why these questions need to be asked. The main purpose of training is learning, and it is that we need to validate. Many other factors that accompany the learning can be assessed

FIGURE 9–7
An Improved Validation Questionnaire

Ellray Associates
Measuring the Results

A. Session: The skills of the effective trainer

(Please place a circle around the number you rate)

       Learned a lot   7 6 5 4 3 2 1   Learned little

If you have circled the range 1 to 4, please say why you have scored at that level.

If you have circled the range 5 to 7, please say how you intend to use this learning.

B. Session: Trainer types

---

without a questionnaire and do not add to the validation of the training. In this example, in addition to the basic rating scales, two questions about the scoring are asked. If low scores, learners are asked to say why they believe there has been little learning. (Perhaps the material was too complex; not broken down into digestible amounts; not relevant; badly presented—none of which would be evident from the scoring alone.

The same question could be asked if the scoring is at the higher end of the scale, but this would reflect a desire on the part of the trainer to receive praise, and thus continue the myth of the happiness sheet. Instead, if the ratings are good and learning has been achieved, this is all we need to know, other than what the learner is going to do with his new learning. If learning has occurred, its translation into the learner's working life is the next important step in the learning cycle.

Some trainers, while agreeing with the principal behind this type of questionnaire, still wish to obtain information/ratings on other aspects of the training—enjoyment, length of sessions, visual aids, the accommodations, and so on. Including such factors increases the number of questions and so decreases the likelihood of obtaining full and honest responses. (There may even be a law of diminishing returns in inverse proportion to the number of questions asked!) If additional questions and scales are included, they should use the format in Figure 9–7. Never present a rating scale alone without also having specific questions requiring answers to justify the rating or the use of the rating.

A COMPREHENSIVE VALIDATION QUESTIONNAIRE

Many of the criteria described so far can be combined when an extensive validation questionnaire needs to be used. In such cases, there is every support for a varied approach, using different methods of obtaining and assessing information. An example is shown in Figure 9–8.

THE THREE-TEST

Before leaving end-of-course validation and its relationship to assessing the effectiveness of the trainer, I want to return to a particular type of questionnaire that was introduced in Chapter Seven: the three-test approach.

As we have seen, traditionally a test is given at the start of the training and repeated at the end of the training—the pre-post-training test. In knowledge and practical training programs, this is a suitable approach showing the change in the learner from "can't do" to (it is hoped) "can do." This approach is not suitable for assessing change in the more subjective training areas and even the practical areas where general skills are being considered. It is particularly inappropriate in such areas as human relations training, interpersonal skills, interviewing training, and even what appear to be specific, objective skills such as negotiating, presentations, and the like. Subjective views based on the models used can be expressed, but these can vary considerably depending on the base used for the expert approach. In many cases, the best that can be done is to ask the learners to assess their own progress. These comments can be compared with the similarly subjective views of the trainer.

Figure 7–1 showed a behavior self-assessment questionnaire that can be administered at the start of an interpersonal skills program to obtain the views of the learners on how they assess their behavioral skills at that stage before training. Let us take one of the items on this questionnaire, which asks them to rate themselves on a scale of 1 to 10 (1 being low) as to "Being aware of my own behavior." One learner might make an entry of 8. This learner considers himself quite aware of his own behavior, but there may be one or two small points of which he is not aware, and that is why he has come to the program.

At the end of the training program, the same questionnaire is administered again, in exactly the same format, but on this occasion, the learners are asked to rate themselves as they see themselves after

FIGURE 9–8
A Comprehensive End-of-Course Questionnaire

Ellray Associates
Options for Trainer's Seminar

---

1. Did you obtain what you hoped for from this seminar? (Please circle the relevant answer.)

   Yes   More than expected   Less than expected   No

2. Whose idea was it that you should attend this seminar? (Please check the relevant answer or answers.)

   No idea   Subordinate
   Superior   Yourself
   Colleague   Other

3. How useful did you find the following activities at the seminar? (Please circle the relevant score.)

   | | Little use | | Lot of use |

   Options relating to the   1 2 3 4 5
   introductory sessions

   If you gave a rating 1, 2, or 3, please state why you have given this rating.

   If you have given a rating 4 or 5, please state how you intend to implement this learning

   | | Little use | | Lot of use |

   The volunteers activity   1 2 3 4 5

   If you gave a rating 1, 2, or 3, please state why you have given this rating.

   If you have given a rating 4 or 5, please state how you intend to use this learning.

4. What specific changes would you suggest to enhance the effectiveness of the course?

5. What was/were the most significant part(s) for you during the seminar? (and why?)

6. What have you learned from the seminar that you intend to put into practice on your return to work?

7. (Answering this question is not mandatory!) Would you attend a seminar on a different subject with this presenter?

---

having been through the program. The initial questionnaire has been retained by the trainer and is not made available at this time to the learner, lest it influence his replies. On this second occasion, our learner might rate the question quoted above as 9. This is the classical pre- and post-test and suggests, although subjectively and from the learner's viewpoint only, that learning has increased by a factor of 10 percent. This may be considered to be low for a weeklong training program designed for people whose interpersonal skills have been assessed by managers as requiring improvement.

The trainer might consequently feel disappointed in the low amount of change and consider that either the material used or his skills left something to be desired.

I suggest that immediately after the second completion, and without reference to either the first or second test, the learners be asked to complete the same questionnaire a third time. On this occasion, they are required to complete the questionnaire as if they were completing it at the start of the training program, but knowing what they now know about the subject of behavior, appropriate behavior, behavior modification, behavior categorization and its meaning, and so on. This suggests, and the learners usually agree with this, that they did not really know where they stood at the beginning of the program because they were not aware of the implications of interpersonal skills—the reason they had come to the program.

At the third completion, the learner might revise his rating for the beginning of the program to 2. As he now rates himself at 9, the increase in self-assessed skill is 70 percent rather than 10 percent—a much healthier change over the learning program! This is still highly subjective, but it is much better than nothing.

ACTION PLANNING

Assessment of the success of a training event, and by inference the effectiveness of the trainer, depends on the learner's commitment to put the learning into action and on his acceptance of the learning and any new concepts. Little commitment to applying new techniques suggests the material is so far out of touch with reality it should not have been introduced (a fault in design and planning by the trainer), was so complex and incomprehensible it is impossible to translate to the work situation (a fault in content design), or was not understood (a fault in the trainer's presentation and awareness).

If, however, the learners make firm commitments to put a number of aspects into operation, the training has been successful and the trainer must be given credit for this. If the action plans include the items initially identified by the trainer as the most significant learning items, and some extra effort was invested in that part of the training, the trainer has obviously been successful in conveying his opinion of its importance. Again, like happiness sheets, it is easy to lead the learners to include in their action plans the items the trainer wants them to include, thus demonstrating his skill. This is equally dishonest on the part of the trainer. The learners should be encouraged and given sufficient time to reflect on the training, consider which factors they believe to be most important and significant to them, and commit themselves in writing to take some positive action. They may not include the factors the trainer believes they should, either from the training content or from his own presentations, but if this is the case, it has to be accepted—this is what the learner must want. Or perhaps the factor on which the trainer thought he was having such an impact may not have appeared in this way at all to the learner—a cause for reflection by the trainer!

My preferred style of action plan sheet is shown in Figure 9–9.

The examples described here are but a few of the many approaches the trainer can take in attempting to validate the training. Some are more valid, some more complex, some more valuable than others, but all try to assess as objectively as possible how effective the training has been from the learner's view. In doing so, the competence of the trainer may also be reflected in the training rating, although we need to ask more questions to define this accurately.

End-of-course validation can be developed into a realistic and effective approach, making the continuance of the "happiness" epithet unjustifiable. But the trainer must stress the importance of validation, allocating sufficient time for forms to be completed in a serious manner and using a measure that demonstrates the learners' views should be, and will be, considered.

As noted above, there are three major reasons a person completing a training program might not implement the knowledge from that session, but there is one more critical component about implementation of the specific training within the working environment that needs to be re-emphasized here. That is the role of the supervisor. If the supervisor is

FIGURE 9–9
Action Planning

Ellray Associates
Action Planning

What I intent to do	How I intend to do it	With what resources	By when

not supportive of the training (because of lack of understanding of the training, belief that the training is wasteful, annoyance with the loss of time for the training and/or lack of involvement with the training department about the training, or any other reason, then the likely use of the knowledge, or skill gained is greatly diminished.

Even the most committed person completing training will not use much of the training knowledge or skill if such action is negatively reinforced by the supervisor.

Since the ultimate goal of any training is to transfer knowledge and/ or skills to an individual for use in the real world, it cannot be mentioned too often that the immediate supervisor of the person being trained is a crucial partner in the learning cycle as it applies to implementation of knowledge.

Chapter Ten

Practical Steps in Trainer Assessment

The preceding chapters have been intended as a gradually developing introduction to this stage of the book where we will look at the steps that can be taken to answer the question, "How do we assess the effectiveness of a trainer?" Even with the information we should already have and other approaches, this is not going to be easy. A number of factors have to be considered, as well as the ways "assessors" look at the direct actions of the trainer.

INITIAL STEPS IN ASSESSMENT

First, as we saw in Chapter One, the place of the trainer within the training organization and the wider employing organization must be recognized—the training quintet. His place in terms of authority, responsibility, and hierarchy must be established to provide a base on which other assessments can be made.

The next requirement that we have as assessors is to determine what kind of "trainer" we are looking at or need to recognize. Is he an on-the-job instructor or a direct instructor, a specific instructions type of trainer or one with a more facilitative brief? There is little value in our assessing an instructor type of trainer if what we are looking for are the skills of a facilitator.

A trainer can be expected to fulfill one or more roles within the training organization and the company. Do we expect him to take on the role of the missionary who is trying to make changes through the training role, or are we seeking an educationalist who will deliver training in the procedures, systems, and methods in existence in terms of "this is what you need to know." Does the trainer need to be so flexible in technique and attitude that he can one day behave in the controlled role of the instructor and the next day in the much more free-ranging role of the human relations facilitator? Again, we must be very clear about the role or roles we are expecting to identify before we set off on the assessment trail.

COMPANY NEEDS

Finally, the demands and requirements of the company must be considered when we are performing the assessment. What role does the company expect the trainer to fulfill? We may assess a trainer who exhibits all the skills of a highly advanced facilitator, group adviser, and group/individual therapist, but all the company requires is a lecturer who will tell the trainees what they have to know and do! How the trainer meets the company's needs would certainly influence our attitude to the trainer under assessment.

The trainer must adopt a similar initial self-assessment for the same reasons. "Am I performing the role not only efficiently and effectively as a trainer, but also the one required of me by the type of training and the company I represent?" If the answer is no, the trainer must ask, "So what am I going to do about it?" If a trainer is carrying out roles and tasks alien to his preferences, attitude, and even skill range, he will be frustrated and eventually there will be a reduction in efficiency and effectiveness. Correction through self-assessment (even if the remedy is to leave the situation to find a more compatible training job) is vastly preferable to having the deficiencies pointed out by an external assessor. Unfortunately, not everybody can take a sufficiently detached point of view to achieve a realistic self-assessment.

SUPPORTIVE EVIDENCE

The training organization may have spent much valuable time on validation analyses of the training, as we saw in the previous two chapters. We saw that information about the skill of the trainer can be gleaned indirectly from these instruments. However, there must always be some circumspection in using these analyses because of all the possible inconsistencies, particularly in the inventories on subjects other than knowledge or practical learning. We would be foolish to ignore such possibly supportive evidence for any other approaches we might take, and a planned program of examining the analyses is an essential part of any assessment program. Installing a training validation program in organizations that lack one will greatly aid the trainer assessment program.

But remember, if the training validation analyses show a satisfactory position, this may not indicate the trainer is the effective item. And if the training analyses suggest little or reduced learning, it does not necessarily mean the trainer is not doing an effective job.

WHAT ARE WE ASSESSING?

When training assessment was introduced, we saw that the basic element in the process was the need to identify the objectives of the training: what the training was setting out to do, and what the trainees/learners would be expected to know/show/do by the end of the training. At the end of the training, tests were administered to check to what extent these objectives had been achieved.

When we are setting out to assess the trainer, a similar approach is necessary. The trainer's objectives must be assessed as well as those of the training. Under normal circumstances, these should be the same; that is, the effective training of or achievement of learning by the people attending the training event or program. This would appear to be self-evident, but there is always a danger that the objectives of the trainer may not coincide with these aims. The trainer's personal objectives may be more self-oriented, and consciously or subconsciously, the trainer may be using the training to satisfy these personal needs.

Identifying personal objectives is difficult for an external assessor; close attention must be paid to what the trainer says and does to seek clues to the "hidden agenda." Usually, indications eventually emerge. The most common problem is when the trainer is being forced to carry out a role that conflicts with his training role preference, and he is unable to come to terms with the demands of the role. A common example of this might be when the trainer has to conduct training events that carry a particular message from the organization to which the trainer is not committed. In such cases, the trainer, overtly or covertly, might try to color the training with his, rather than the organization's, views.

TRAINER NEEDS ASSESSMENT

Linking the objectives of the trainer and the training/trainees is the identification of needs. Meaningful training starts with a complete and accurate identification of the training population's needs and whether the suggested training fits in with these needs. It is similar with the trainer. What are his needs?

In Chapter Three, the general skills of a trainer were considered. These were sufficient to identify the general role and skill/knowledge/attitude needs of the trainer, but assessment requires much more specific information about the presence and absence of these factors. This information can be obtained in a number of ways, ranging from the relatively simple task description to the more comprehensive, holistic description of the competences required by a trainer.

TRAINER TASK ANALYSIS

The first example of trainer task analysis is relatively simple to complete and can be used as a self-assessment instrument or as an assessment guide by an external assessor. The full instrument is as follows.

An Inventory of Trainer Skills

The purpose of this inventory is to help you assess your skills (or assess the skills of another) in a number of training aspects. The emphasis is on the presentation of training sessions, which is the more common activity of many trainers, but the list can be extended to include other types of activity. The results will indicate strengths and weaknesses in your training role, for which you may take developmental action. The inventory will be of use only if you complete it honestly and realistically; complete it as you know the situation is rather than how you would like it to be. Go through the inventory twice. The first time, mark each item in accordance with how you see the present situation. Then go over the list again and identify the priority items that are indicated as your having to take some action. Take the necessary action on these, then return to the list to take any necessary further action.

	No Problem or Not Relevant	Satisfactory	Should Improve	Must Improve
1. Listening actively	_____	_____	_____	_____
2. Expressing myself clearly	_____	_____	_____	_____

3. Being brief and concise _____ _____ _____ _____
4. Taking up views expressed _____ _____ _____ _____
5. Using relevant humor _____ _____ _____ _____
6. Using real-life anecdotes _____ _____ _____ _____
7. Avoiding jargon _____ _____ _____ _____
8. Fitting my language to the learner _____ _____ _____ _____
9. Using my voice efficiently _____ _____ _____ _____
10. Helping learners understand the difficult points _____ _____ _____ _____
11. Not forcing my own views in discussion _____ _____ _____ _____
12. Asking open questions _____ _____ _____ _____
13. Answering questions effectively _____ _____ _____ _____
14. Using appropriate non-verbals and gestures _____ _____ _____ _____
15. Identifying the learners' learning preference style _____ _____ _____ _____
16. Using relevant visual aids _____ _____ _____ _____
17. Using clear and readable visual aids _____ _____ _____ _____
18. Using clear, readable writing on posters _____ _____ _____ _____
19. Adding all comments by learners to posters _____ _____ _____ _____
20. Using videos when relevant _____ _____ _____ _____
21. Using videos effectively _____ _____ _____ _____
22. Always following up videos with some action _____ _____ _____ _____
23. Use of other visual aids _____ _____ _____ _____
24. Able to use range of techniques and methods _____ _____ _____ _____
25. Being aware of group's behavior _____ _____ _____ _____
26. Being aware of own behavior _____ _____ _____ _____
27. Giving instructions effectively _____ _____ _____ _____
28. Being enthusiastic _____ _____ _____ _____
29. Coping with conflict within the group _____ _____ _____ _____
30. Coping with conflict between me and group _____ _____ _____ _____

31. Handling difficult
    participants   _____   _____   _____   _____
32. Handling too high con-
    tributing participants _____   _____   _____   _____
33. Handling too quiet
    participants   _____   _____   _____   _____
34. Knowing how to "mix"
    groups effectively   _____   _____   _____   _____
35. Holding the interest of
    a group   _____   _____   _____   _____
36. Setting up activities
    effectively   _____   _____   _____   _____
37. Taking feedback after
    activities   _____   _____   _____   _____
38. Commenting appropri-
    ately after case study
    interviews   _____   _____   _____   _____
39. Being able to introduce
    spontaneous input
    sessions   _____   _____   _____   _____
40. Being able to radically
    modify program during
    the event to satisfy the
    needs of the learners   _____   _____   _____   _____
41. Other training activities
    not included in above. _____   _____   _____   _____

Completion of this inventory is not an exacting task, but it can provide considerable information on which to base developmental consideration and prepare assessors and self-assessors for more comprehensive inventories.

TRAINER TASK INVENTORY

The most useful and commonly used comprehensive inventory relating to the tasks of trainers is the "Trainer Task Inventory." This is based on original work in the Air Transport and Travel Industry Training Board by Terry Morgan and Martin Costello. When the board became defunct, the work was at field trial stage, and the British Training Agency (then the Manpower Services Commission) funded Morgan and Costello to complete the work. As a result of further cooperation between the Manpower Services Commission and the Institute for

Training and Development, the inventory was completed and published in June 1984.

The Trainer Task Inventory (TTI) is essentially a structured task analysis consisting of a list of all the tasks carried out by trainers. The tasks are organized into family groups of related tasks, but not necessarily with a particular jobholder's role. The flexibility within the TTI enables it to be applied to a variety of trainer roles, with suitable additions and omissions to make the inventory relevant to each. The TTI can be completed by the jobholders or by their manager on an assessment/identification basis.

USES OF THE TTI

Because of the comprehensive nature of the TTI, a number of applications have been suggested for it, in addition to assessing the tasks of a training jobholder.

Planning

The TTI can help in career choice for people who may be considering entering the profession and want to have some idea of the range of work that would be involved.

Recruitment

This follows from the planning function in that if potential employees are to be encouraged to come to an organization, the more useful information they are given, the better for both the recruiter and the applicant. A job and task analysis should be performed in any recruitment exercise to enable a job profile to be established. From this, a preferred person profile is produced to enable the recruiters to compare the candidates with the job requirements.

Organization

The inventory has a use in determining the structuring of the individual jobs and the overall role requirements of that department. This is particularly useful when a new department has to be set up, although it is equally valuable when an existing department has to be assessed or inspected for validity.

Self-assessment

Because the inventory is sufficiently comprehensive to describe what a trainer should be able to do, an honest self-assessment approach can be achieved to help the jobholder decide what steps are necessary in his self-development.

Appraisal

The self-assessment and development approach can be linked readily with the annual appraisal system. One of the common failures of appraisal systems is that the appraiser has nothing against which to assess the capabilities and competence of the person under appraisal. The TTI can help identify what should be within the jobholder's repertoire, which leaves the appraiser to assess the level to which these are being achieved.

Role Descriptions

The TTI is an extensive instrument that requires time and resources, both on the part of the trainers and their managers, but once completed, it provides a description of all the job processes in the department. As roles and jobs change, it is relatively simple to update the TTIs with slight amendments.

Discipline

Although not the intention of the originators of the TTI, it can be used in the discipline process. If the need for discipline arises because of work failings, a probation period is usually set during which the "offender" is required to improve. The TTI can help to identify areas in which there should be competence and point to those that will be looked at closely during the probation period.

THE TTI AND ASSESSMENT

The main use of TTI is in the assessment of the skills of trainers. It provides at the minimum a listing of the tasks a trainer should be capable of doing, which can be molded to relate directly to whatever trainer role is required. As will be seen later, the level of use of the TTI is very flexible, ranging from a simple can/can't do approach to a more sophisticated one that considers other competence levels.

THE STRUCTURES OF THE TTI

The TTI is based on the three major levels of activity in a trainer's task, plus a fourth one concerned with a variety of general principles.

The three levels of activity are:

- Helping people to learn and develop.
- Helping people to solve performance problems.
- Helping people to anticipate needs and problems and formulate policies.

Emphasis is on the trainer's role in helping the learners with whom he comes into contact. As we have seen throughout this book, there must also be full awareness of the organization's needs. The needs of the organization are reflected in the needs of the individual, otherwise the individual does not have a place in the organization. This may appear to be a harsh observation, but previous consideration has shown that if the two needs are not in balance, the training of the learners will suffer and hence the learners (and consequently the organization) will be the losers.

Helping people to learn and develop includes identifying learning and training needs; designing and preparing for the training events; instructing/training either face to face with individuals or groups or at a distance with other methods; and evaluating the training provided.

Helping people to solve performance problems involves taking the necessary action to identify problems among the target population; selecting and designing appropriate intervening strategies; implementing the intervention; and evaluating the results of the interventions. In the TTI parlance, an *intervention* is "any activity undertaken to overcome an identified problem."

Helping people to anticipate needs and problems and to formulate policies relates to identifying future needs and problems and formulating strategies and plans to deal with these.

The final activity was labeled *general functions* and included all factors that would support some or all of the other activities—administration, management, knowing the organization, and self-development.

When compared with the skills of an effective trainer as considered earlier in this book, a number of factors appear to be missing. One of the main advantages of the TTI is its flexibility; necessary elements of a particular trainer's job can always be added later. One criticism that can be leveled at the TTI is the absence of guidance on the personal behavioral aspects required in the job; effectiveness does not necessarily imply completely appropriate behavior. As subsequent competence assessors have discovered, this is the "black hole" of assessment and one that causes most discussion.

The structure of the TTI is progressive; whether you look at the progression from the bottom to the top or top to bottom is not too relevant. The TTI takes the latter course and describes

- The four levels of activity briefly described above.
- A number of work areas within each level of activity.
- A number of task groups (or tasks) within each work area.

The TTI contains four levels of activity, 17 work areas distributed unevenly throughout the levels, and 252 tasks, with spaces for additional task entries. It is not possible to include here the complete document, copies of which can be obtained from the Institute of Training and Development, but the following gives the flavor of the format.

TTI FORMAT

The first level of activity, which is concerned with "helping people to learn and develop," is subdivided into seven work areas, each work area having from 4 to 23 task groups.

As an example, work area 4 is concerned with preparing for training/learning events and contains the following 23 task groups.

1. Write/update manuals.
2. Write programmed texts.
3. Write handouts.
4. Design visual aids—overheads, etc.
5. Make visual aids—overheads, etc.
6. Design audiovisual aids (videos/films).
7. Make audiovisual aids (videos/films).
8. Set up and position audiovisual equipment.
9. Repair damaged equipment.

10. Purchase training material.
11. Negotiate resources/training facilities in hotels.
12. Choose outside speakers.
13. Brief outside speakers.
14. Conduct pre-course interviews with trainees.
15. Send out joining instructions.
16. Analyze pre-course reports on trainees by their supervisors.
17. Test alternative methods/media.
18. Write case studies.
19. Investigate ready-made courses/materials.
20. Design trainee self-assessment instruments.
21. Develop computer-managed instruction material.
22. Prepare tape/slide script material.
23. Design tape/slide visual material.
24. —
25. —
26. —
27. —
28. —
29. —
30. —

A number of these tasks are not relevant to some trainers, whereas other trainers will say immediately there are a number of omissions when they consider their own jobs. The former need only delete those items that are not relevant to them, and the latter add in the spaces provided the tasks that relate to them and are not shown.

Consequently, when an individual TTI is completed, there should be considerably more than the original 252 tasks or considerably fewer. For example, when I was employed in one organization as a direct management training trainer, I was not concerned at all with tasks 2, 9, 11, 12, 13, 15, and 21, although there were at least eight other tasks I could have added to the list. This is the way the TTI is intended to be used; it is not a definitive document.

USING THE TTI

The flexibility of the TTI is not restricted to the task group entries, but there are a number of ways it can be used. The start of an actual page (in fact, the one from which the task groups listed above were taken) is in the following format. It contains one method of using the inventory.

Work area 4: *Preparing for training/learning events*	1	2	3	4
Listed below is a task group and the tasks it includes. Check all tasks you perform. Add at the bottom any tasks you do that are not listed.				
Task Group	if done			

1. Write/update manuals
etc.

In the example shown, the trainer is invited to place a check in column 1 against all the tasks performed and to add any that are not shown. If one of the tasks is not performed, no check is placed in column 1. The immediate question raised by this omission is, "Is this part of the job that should be performed and therefore action has to be taken to allow it to be checked?" This is an immediate assessment, not necessarily of the trainer's competence, but one that identifies what he should be doing. The remaining columns offer options to the uses of the TTI.

One approach I have found particularly useful is to use the TTI not only to identify tasks that should be performed, but also to identify the level of competence attained (or at least a subjective assessment of this). Instead of four columns, I use only one, although there are variations that can use more than the one column. Delete all the tasks that are not relevant and add those that have not been included.

When this has been done, work through all the entries and against each entry mark either a check, a cross, an asterisk, a zero, or any other preferred mark. If the competence level is nonexistent, make no mark. If that aspect is known, but at a superficial level only, place one mark; if it is known or is at a skill level above the superficial level, but not to such an extent that the person would be capable of performing it effectively, place two marks; if the person could perform it effectively or satisfactorily, place three marks; if there is complete competence, four marks. A look down one column will then immediately show where strengths and weaknesses, competences, and training needs lie. If columns are retained, each column can be used for a different level of competence and the "dog-leg" picture that emerges will show strengths and weaknesses clearly.

The published TTI describes other uses that have been introduced by some organizations. The U.S. Air Force, from whose original work the TTI was developed, uses column one as shown—that the task has been

completed. Column 2 is devoted to time spent on the task and a grading
of 1 to 7 is used here. Column 3 also has a seven-point coded scale concerned with importance.

Other options used have been:

1. Column 1 is marked if the task has been performed in the past 18 months.

    Column 2 is marked if the task has been carried out in the past 18 months
              but the trainer believes it should not be tackled by them.

    Column 3 is marked if the task has not been carried out in the past 18
              months, but the trainer believes it should be tackled by them.

    Column 4 is marked if the trainer believes they need further training or
              guidance.

2. Column 1 is marked if the task is completed.

    Column 2 is marked if the task is not being tackled but should be part of
              the job.

    Column 3 is marked if the task is being tackled but should not be part of
              the job.

These examples demonstrate the flexibility of the TTI and the fact that
it can be used in a variety of ways, depending on your needs.

The TTI can itself be used as a simple checklist when a trainer is self-
assessing or a trainer is being assessed by an external assessor. Either use
demands that a basic document showing the full extent (and constraints)
of the job should have been completed and agreed on; this defines the job
against which any assessment can be made. It must be appreciated, however, that the TTI is used to assess tasks and their performance more than
as a means of assessing the competence level within a particular task or
operation, but it gives the assessor an inventory of what can then be assessed for competence.

COMPETENCE STANDARDS

The TTI, although a valuable and useful inventory and one that serves its
purpose well, is in many ways a crude device. The British government
has attempted to develop national standards for all occupations and used
a functional analysis as the basis because it looks at the whole job rather
than concentrating on the tasks. The first definition in the analysis is that
competence is "the ability to perform activities within an occupation to
the standards expected." After this definition comes the identification of
a manager's role in progressively detailed terms.

THE KEY PURPOSE

The start of the description is the key purpose, which, in terms of the manager's role, is "to achieve the organization's objective and continuously improve its performance." This purpose must be at the heart of every manager's job. However important this statement might be, it must be more specific to make assessment of the standards possible.

THE KEY ROLE

The next level of a manager's job is determined by what are described as the key roles. There are the discrete areas of responsibility, and for a "generic" manager have been defined as:

- Managing operations.
- Managing finance.
- Managing people.
- Managing information.
- Personal competences.

These key roles are the forces by which the key purpose is achieved and describe how it will be achieved, but still not with sufficient detail to enable assessment.

UNITS

Units are the basic building blocks of the functional analysis on which the standards are universally determined and follow naturally from the key roles.

Each key role contains a number of units, the actual number varying from one key role to another, depending on its complexity. For example, the key role relating to the financial responsibilities of a manager contains two units:

- Monitor and control the use of resources.
- Secure effective resources allocation for activities and projects.

Other roles break down into different number of units; for example, managing people has four units.

ELEMENTS

The statements of roles and units describe "what" a manager does, rather than "how." This more detailed description is left to the elements into which each unit is divided. For example, two elements are involved in the unit concerned with monitoring and controlling the use of resources (each unit contains a number of elements, again depending on the complexity of the work). The elements in our example unit are:

- Control costs and enhance value.
- Monitor and control activities against budgets.

PERFORMANCE CRITERIA

The next step is to detail how the success of these objectives or the competence of the manager can be examined and assessed. Other factors are necessary for a full assessment, but a set of performance criteria takes the assessment a considerable distance. Once again, the preceding levels are divided into a number of parts, the number depending on the complexity of the work. If we take the element that requires the manager to monitor and control activities against budget, the performance criteria to check the competence include:

- Expenditure is within agreed limits, does not compromise future spending requirements, and conforms to the organization's policy and procedures.
- Requests for expenditure outside the manager's responsibility are referred promptly to the appropriate people.
- Where appropriate, expenditures are phased in accordance with a planned time scale.

And so on to a total of eight criteria.

RANGE INDICATORS

The final detail that must be considered relates to the variations that can occur within an occupation. If all these were included in the main body of the statement, it would become too extensive and too detailed to be a

usable document. Instead, in any set of standards, the basic generic elements are shown, but all the possible variations are included under the
title "range indicators" (originally called "range statements").

Using our element example of "Monitor and control activities against
budgets," the relevant range indicators include:

- Monitoring relates to an accounting center for which the manager
  has responsibility.
- Monitoring
  1. Direct costs of materials, staffing, expenses.
  2. Relevant overhead charges.
  3. Any revenue earned by the accounting center.
  4. Cash flow.
- Expenditure outside the manager's area of responsibility will be
  due to it
  1. Being over stated budget limits.
  2. Subject to other organizational controls.

and so on.

The draft statement of key purpose, key roles, units, and elements for
the occupation standards for managers (middle managers II) is shown in
Figure 10–1. The set of performance criteria and range indicators for one
of the elements is shown in Figure 10–2.

TRAINER STANDARDS KEY ROLES, UNITS, AND ELEMENTS

The key purpose of training and development is to "develop human potential to assist organizations and individuals to achieve their objectives." Within this, five key areas in training and development have
been identified:

A   Identify training and development needs.

B   Design training and development strategies and plans.

C   Provide learning opportunities resources and support.

D   Evaluate the effectiveness of training and development.

E   Support training and development advances and practice.

Each key area or principal function is subdivided into either two or
three key roles identified by the codes A1, A2, B1, B2, and so on. For

FIGURE 10–1
Occupational Standards for Managers (Management II)

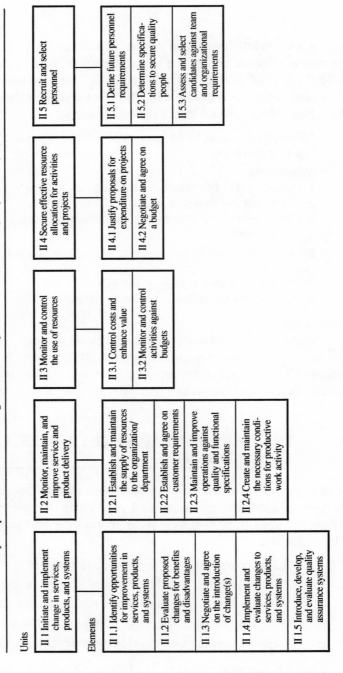

Key Purpose: *To achieve the organization's objectives and continuously improve its performance*

Units

| II 6 Develop teams, individuals, and self to enhance performance | II 7 Plan, allocate, and evaluate work carried out by teams, individuals, and self | II 8 Create and maintain effective working relationships | II 9 Seek, evaluate, and organize information for action | II 10 Exchange information to solve problems and make decisions |

Elements

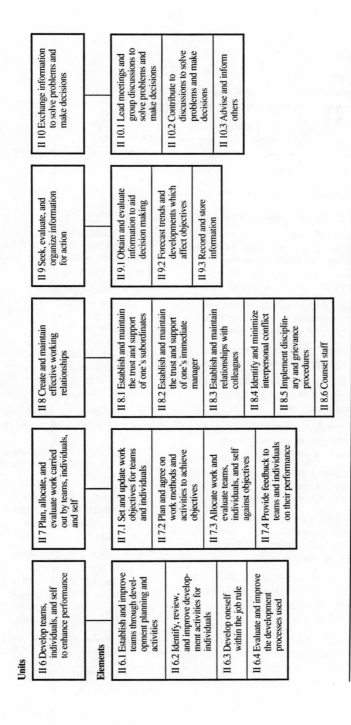

II 6.1 Establish and improve teams through development planning and activities	II 7.1 Set and update work objectives for teams and individuals	II 8.1 Establish and maintain the trust and support of one's subordinates	II 9.1 Obtain and evaluate information to aid decision making	II 10.1 Lead meetings and group discussions to solve problems and make decisions
II 6.2 Identify, review, and improve development activities for individuals	II 7.2 Plan and agree on work methods and activities to achieve objectives	II 8.2 Establish and maintain the trust and support of one's immediate manager	II 9.2 Forecast trends and developments which affect objectives	II 10.2 Contribute to discussions to solve problems and make decisions
II 6.3 Develop oneself within the job rule	II 7.3 Allocate work and evaluate teams, individuals, and self against objectives	II 8.3 Establish and maintain relationships with colleagues	II 9.3 Record and store information	II 10.3 Advise and inform others
II 6.4 Evaluate and improve the development processes used	II 7.4 Provide feedback to teams and individuals on their performance	II 8.4 Identify and minimize interpersonal conflict		
		II 8.5 Implement disciplinary and grievance procedures		
		II 8.6 Counsel staff		

Source: Reproduced with permission of the Department of Employment's Training, Education and Enterprise Division

FIGURE 10–2
Occupational Standards for Mangers (Management II)

---

*Key Purpose: To achieve the organization's objectives and
continuously improve its performance*

Key Role: Manage Finance

Unit II 3 Monitor and control the use of resources

Element II 3.2 Monitor and control activities against budgets

Performance Criteria:

(a) Expenditure is within agreed limits, does not compromise future spending requirements and conforms to the organizations's policy and procedures

(b) Requests for expenditure outside the manager's responsibility are referred promptly to the appropriate people

(c) Where appropriate, expenditure is phased in accordance with a planned time scale

(d) Actual income and expenditure is checked against agreed budgets at regular, appropriate intervals

(e) Where a budget shortfall is likely to occur, the appropriate people are informed with minimum delay

(f) Any necessary authority for changes in allocation between budget heads is obtained in advance of requirement

(g) Any modifications to agreed budgets during the accounting period are consistant with agreed guidelines and correctly authorized.

(h) Prompt, corrective action is taken where necessary in response to significant deviations from budget

Range Indicators:

Monitor relates to an accounting center for which the manager has responsibility.

Monitoring covers:
• direct costs of:
    materials
    staffing
    expenses
• relevant overhead charges
• any revenue earned by the accounting center
• cash flow.

Expenditure outside the manager's area of responsibility will be due to it:
• being over stated budget limits
• subject to other organizational controls.

The manager authorizes expenditure in accordance with the organization's financial procedures.

Corrective action includes:
• advising subordinates to alter/ modify their activities
• altering budget allocations within the limits of responsibility
• rescheduling expenditures.

Source: Reproduced with permission of the Department of Employment's Training, Education and Enterprise Division

example, key role A1 is "identify organizational requirements for training and development"; A2 is "identify the learning needs of individuals and groups." Figure 10–3 summarizes all the key roles contained in the standards.

Training and development standards are broken down into more detailed elements in the same way that the generic manager standards were subdivided from the key role level.

Key role A1 has three units of performance:

A11 Agree and obtain support for the contribution of training and development in organizational strategy.

A12 Identify organizational training and development needs.

A13 Agree on priorities for developing the training and development function.

Other key roles have similarly associated units of performance and these are given in Figure 10–3. If we follow key role A1 through the standards we see (Figure 10–4) that unites A11, A12, and A13 each has between two and four elements of performance; these are coded A111, A112; A121, A122, A123, A124; A131, A132, A133. Unit A11, which is "agree and obtain support for the contribution of training and development to organizational strategy," contains two elements, A111 and A112.

A111 states: "Agree the contribution of training and development to organizational strategy."

A112 states: "Promote and support decision makers' commitment to the agreed contribution of training and development."

Figure 10–5 describes these two elements and the two other aspects of standards—performance criteria and range indicators.

The performance criteria are the practical aids to assessing competence in training and development. In effect, they are the questions from which it can be decided whether the respondent can do the function involved. The number of criteria reflects the complexity of the element of performance. Both elements A111 and A112, for example, have seven performance criteria each. Other elements have more, others less.

In addition to the performance criteria, each element has a number of range indicators (also shown in Figure 10–5). The range indicators can be used to vary the standards and define the range of applications of the element—that is, the types of relationships, resources, methods, processes, and locations—for which achievement of the specified outcomes

FIGURE 10–3
Training and Development Key Purpose, Areas, Key Roles, and Units of Performance

Standards – Framework

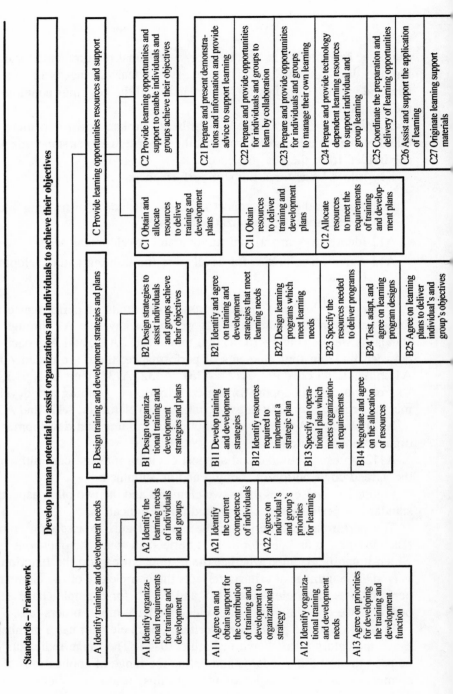

Standards – Framework

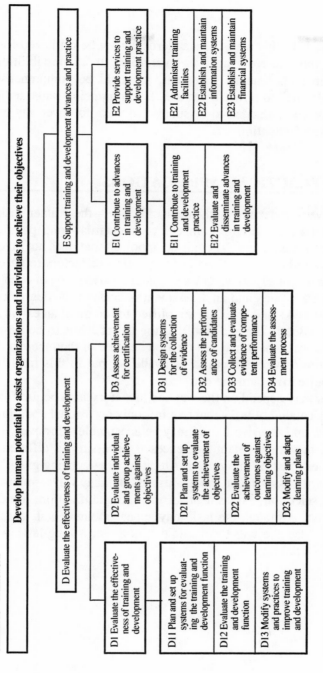

Develop human potential to assist organizations and individuals to achieve their objectives

D Evaluate the effectiveness of training and development

E Support training and development advances and practice

D1 Evaluate the effectiveness of training and development

D11 Plan and set up systems for evaluating the training and development function

D12 Evaluate the training and development function

D13 Modify systems and practices to improve training and development

D2 Evaluate individual and group achievements against objectives

D21 Plan and set up systems to evaluate the achievement of objectives

D22 Evaluate the achievement of outcomes against learning objectives

D23 Modify and adapt learning plans

D3 Assess achievement for certification

D31 Design systems for the collection of evidence

D32 Assess the performance of candidates

D33 Collect and evaluate evidence of competent performance

D34 Evaluate the assessment process

E1 Contribute to advances in training and development

E11 Contribute to training and development practice

E12 Evaluate and disseminate advances in training and development

E2 Provide services to support training and development practice

E21 Administer training facilities

E22 Establish and maintain information systems

E23 Establish and maintain financial systems

is required. In this way, the standards cannot be criticized for being too narrow and not covering every variation. If all possibilities were included in one standard statement, it would be comprehensive, but it would also be too unwieldy to use. By introducing range indicators, the standards can be added to or subtracted from to cover any training and development situation.

PRACTICAL APPLICATIONS

Whichever turns out to be the most effective—the Trainer Task Inventory described earlier or the competence standards—one painful fact will have become apparent. There is no approach that does not involve a complex and perhaps exceptionally long listing of factors to be considered. This is particularly so when we consider a varied type of occupation such as that of a trainer, and an assessment is made of the degree of complexity. If the tasks and roles are simplified to too great an extent, there may be little value in the end result. If the list of items to be assessed is too long, the instrument may not be used because of the inherent difficulties. Compromises would seem to be available, but in this field this may be more ineffective than the extremes.

Much may depend on the way the inventory is to be used. If it is to be simply a catalog of tasks that requires only occasional updating and modification, an extensive listing may be acceptable. However, if a working instrument with constant references is necessary, a different format of guidelines must be introduced. Attention is now being given to analysis, which, with assessment, can be utilized in many ways—recruitment, appraisal, selection, assessment for job and qualification, job description, and so on. Although the task may appear monumental, once produced, and provided the will to maintain it is there, a long-lasting instrument will be available.

FIGURE 10–4
Training and Development Units and Elements

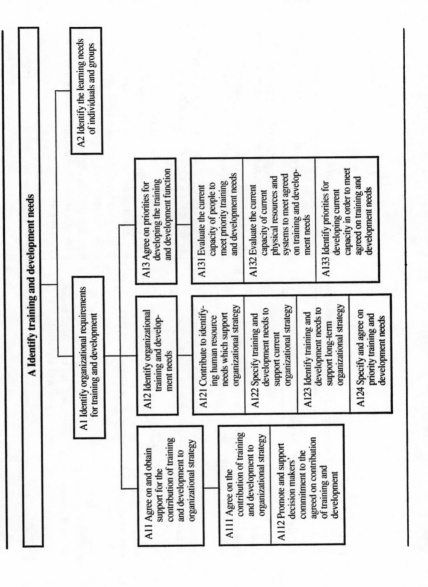

A Identify training and development needs

A1 Identify organizational requirements for training and development

A2 Identify the learning needs of individuals and groups

A11 Agree on and obtain support for the contribution of training and development to organizational strategy

A111 Agree on the contribution of training and development to organizational strategy

A112 Promote and support decision makers' commitment to the agreed on contribution of training and development

A12 Identify organizational training and development needs

A121 Contribute to identifying human resource needs which support organizational strategy

A122 Specify training and development needs to support current organizational strategy

A123 Identify training and development needs to support long-term organizational strategy

A124 Specify and agree on priority training and development needs

A13 Agree on priorities for developing the training and development function

A131 Evaluate the current capacity of people to meet priority training and development needs

A132 Evaluate the current capacity of current physical resources and systems to meet agreed on training and development needs

A133 Identify priorities for developing current capacity in order to meet agreed on training and development needs

FIGURE 10–5
Training and Development Elements, Performance Criteria, and Range Indicators

A11 Agree and Obtain Support for the Contribution of Training and Development to Organizational Strategy A1

A111 Agree the contribution of training and development to organizational strategy

a. Proposals are presented that identify relevant training and development contributions that support organizational strategy

b. Where relevant, proposals are based on evaluations of previous contributions of training and development to organizational policy

c. Proposals match training and development options to organizational policies

d. Options that have the greatest potential for success are recommended and promoted

e. Policy makers are given opportunities to ask questions and seek clarification

f. Negotiations and agreements are conducted and concluded in a manner that promotes and maintains goodwill and trust

g. Agreed options are accurately summarized and made available to those who need the information

A112 Promote and support decision makers' commitment to the agreed contribution of training and development

a. The relationship between training and development's agreed contribution and the priorities of decision makers is accurately identified

b. Presentations are made to decision makers that clearly identify and realistically evaluate the agreed contribution of training and development

c. Accurate and appropriate analyses of added value and costs and benefits of training and development are made available to decision makers

d. Nontangible benefits are identified, accurately and realistically evaluated, and promoted to decision makers

e. Relevant examples of positive organizational outcomes from training and development are identified and made available to decision makers

f. Decision makers are given opportunities to ask questions and seek clarification

g. The information and support required by decision makers in order for them to promote training and development is sought from them agreed, and provided

Range Indicators

Organizational strategies: proactive/supply led; reactive/demand led

Relationship with policy makers; peer/subordinate/superior: inside/outside own organization: employer/employee/client

Sources of evidence for options: internal/external; research and survey reports/professional and trade press

Training and development options

Presentation methods: oral, written, audiovisual, computer-based

Presentation/negotiation processes: direct/face to face; remote/via systems (such as teleconferencing systems)

Range Indicators

Sources for priorities: business plans/ reports; performance reports (formal/informal); anecdotal data; formal/informal data collection

Relationship with decision makers: peer/subordinate/superior: inside/outside own organization: employer/employee/client:

Organizational benefits: quantative/qualitative: organizational mission: competitive advantage:

Management of skill supply: impact on local/national/ international economy: impact on local/national/international community

Sources of evidence and examples: research: organizational reports and records: networks: professional organizations/journals

Presentation methods: oral, written, audiovisual, computer-based

Presentation/dissemination processes: direct/face to face: indirect (such as reports, discussion papers/newsletters): remote/via systems (such as teleconferencing systems)

Types of support to decision makers: information: materials: equipment: facilities: administrative/professional services

Source: Figures 10–3, 10–4, and 10–5 are reproduced here with the permission of the Employment Department, TEED, from the TDLB "National Standards for Training and Development" (Employment Department, January 1991.)

Chapter Eleven

Trainer Assessment in Action

All the ingredients for the assessment of a trainer have now been described with the exception of two:

- Assessment planning.
- Assessment instrumentation.

These two factors play a major role in the approach taken to assess a trainer. As in the earlier sections of this book, the need for effective planning is crucial if the task is to be completed successfully. This is as true for the assessment of a trainer as it is for the training itself.

Unfortunately, for a variety of reasons, trainer assessment is not given the planning accorded to training events themselves—often because of the pull on the training department and trainers to continue with additional training events.

As noted earlier, it is virtually impossible to eliminate the subjectivity of evaluation in assessing trainers, but approaching the assessment process in the same way as you would approach a training event greatly enhances the quality and viability of the assessment. Given the potential personnel issues, as well as the potential impact on productivity of the individual trainer and the training efforts, it is no longer possible to just schedule a meeting with a trainer and begin a review process.

A plan, much like a strategic plan, is needed that outlines the process to be used. The plan needs to address the critical questions, "who, what, when, where, and why." These are the elements that any journalism student or reporter will tell you need to be answered to develop a good story. The same can be said for the evaluation process.

WHO

The first step in assessing a trainer is to determine who will conduct the assessment. This may seem very basic, but it is not. A number of options are available as to who can conduct the assessment, but each one has both its pluses and minuses.

Two crucial elements are needed by the person conducting the assessment. First, the person needs to understand the basics of training—methods, techniques, approaches, design, and so on. Second, the person needs to have some link to the person being assessed.

In a large training department or organization, the logical choice might be the training manager or supervisor of the department. In some cases, this person might not have the knowledge of the basics of training. Many training departments are supervised by people with titles such as director of personnel or human resources. That person's background may have nothing to do with training, and if there is no knowledge of the process, then the evaluation will be of little value. If, on the other hand, this person is or has been a trainer, then it would appear that this individual is the ideal person to conduct the assessment since he has both the knowledge of the basics of training and the direct line authority.

Despite what appears to be a perfect blend for the assessor, such a situation can produce less than quality reviews unless certain precautions are taken. For instance, if the assessor is a trainer and the person being assessed is approaching the training material in a way that differs from that of the assessor, there is a tendency for the person doing the assessment to say, "I conducted this training in a different way," which translates in terms of the assessment into, "I conducted this training in a *better* way." Also, if the person conducting the assessment is responsible for developing training material and the trainer is presenting such material during the evaluation, the tendency is to attribute any problems during the training to the trainer, not the material.

It is crucial that the person conducting the assessment understand the biases he brings to the evaluation.

This problem is not unique to a supervisor who is also a trainer. Many corporations employ outside training consulting firms to assess their trainers. These people generally have clear knowledge of training methods and approaches, but are often challenged in their assessments on issues directly related to corporate mission, corporate environment, and so on.

Training, as noted in earlier sections, is not conducted in a vacuum, but rather needs to be tied directly to a corporate need and corporate mission. All of the corporate environmental factors must be considered within the assessment process since they bear directly on the ability of the trainer to conduct the training. When an outside firm is used for assessment, it is unlikely it has an in-depth understanding of the corporate environment; therefore, it is crucial that a strong link to the individual trainer be established through the enhancement of the outside assessor by the supervisor or upper management of the corporation.

Some firms approach assessment of trainers by providing management level non-trainers with a solid understanding of the principles and methods of training and then having them conduct the assessment. This eliminates a lot of trainer approach bias issues and allows for linkage to upper management levels, thus making it a valuable option. One note of caution should be sounded, however. Using this approach requires training the non-trainers, and often the task of developing and conducting this particular training falls to the training department, meaning the trainers are responsible for training those who will assess them.

There are other options. Assessment can be conducted by peer trainers or can be a self-assessment by the trainer himself.

In the peer assessment process, another trainer observes and assesses the trainer. When peer assessors are used, there is clear knowledge of the principles of training and even a clear understanding of the corporate environment within which the the training event occurs, but peer constraint must be considered in the assessment. Generally, when peer assessment is used, the one being assessed turns around and assesses the one who assessed him.

Peer assessment is very valuable when it is coupled with an additional assessor. Having two assessments tends to balance the assessment and allows for focusing on issues that were brought out in both assessments. This multiple assessment has many advantages, especially if one of the assessors is a non-trainer and the other is a trainer. The biggest problem with multiple assessors is having an additional person observe the actual training event.

Self-assessment is not uncommon when the training department comprises only one person. The only way that person can evaluate the training in many cases is through self-assessment. A vast majority of trainers conduct self-assessment regularly to improve their training skills. It is important that the trainer approach the self-assessment in the same way he would approach assessing another trainer.

Since observation is impossible in the direct sense, a videotape of the presentation, which can be reviewed later, can substitute for an actual in-action observation. One important thing in self-assessment is that the trainer complete a TTI before the assessment so he is aware of the areas in which a bias exists.

With all of the precautions mentioned for each form of assessment, it is difficult to determine who is the best choice to conduct an assessment of a trainer. The options are several, and circumstances, interest, cost, and timing generally determine the method that will be used.

The obvious options, as outlined earlier, are:

- The manager or supervisor.
- A non-trainer, but knowledgeable manager from the corporation.
- An outside training consultant or firm.
- A peer assessor from within the training department or corporation.
- A self-assessment.

One form of assessment has not yet been addressed and that is trainee assessment. This was not mentioned in the listing above because trainee assessment is very unreliable. Ironically, it is one of the most common forms of trainer assessment in use today. We have all been to training sessions where we are asked to rate, among other things, the performance of the trainer.

Trainee assessment is probably the worst option and least valuable assessment tool that can be used in assessing a trainer's effectiveness. This is true for a number of reasons, but the most important is that the trainees are too intimately involved with the training to be able to judge the effectiveness of the trainer.

This deep involvement clouds the ability of the trainees to assess the skills of the trainer, and the personal feelings of the trainees for the trainer will influence their comments. Strong positive feelings toward a trainer are often referred to as "training euphoria," and the resulting assessment lacks neutrality.

In addition, as was noted, one of the important needs in assessing a trainer is understanding the principles of training. This is not likely to be the case with the majority of trainees, so they also lack one of the basic criteria for good assessment.

The views of the trainees should be considered, especially as it relates to the training content, but the information should be treated as supplemental to the assessment rather than as the assessment.

As can be seen, selecting who will conduct the trainer assessment is not easy if the desire is to develop as good an assessment as possible. There is real value in more input, so multiple assessments should be considered. At the least, consideration should be given to self-assessment as well as whatever other form of assessor is selected.

A few notes to consider:

- If the assessment is being conducted by another trainer or an outside consultant, have the individual complete a TTI (see Chapter 9) before the assessment so he is aware of biases that may influence the assessment.
- If self-assessment is being used, ensure that the same process that would be used for an assessment of another is used for self-assessment, including completion of a TTI.
- Trainee assessment should be used as supplemental material or in combination with another form of assessment.
- Most importantly, it must always be remembered that we are assessing a subjective event and therefore there will always be value judgments made by the assessor.

WHAT

Once the who has been decided, the next step is the what. *What* defines the boundaries within which the assessment will occur. The assessment will be designed for a specific purpose and that will indicate what items need to be included in the assessment. These items can include: development and design of a training module, presentation of material, use of audiovisual aids, interactive events, and so on. The purpose of the assessment must be understood to proceed with an effective assessment.

Observation becomes a major tool in those issues that relate to interaction between the trainer and the trainees, such as presentation of material, interactive events (role-playing), use of audiovisual materials, and others that require an actual training environment to be assessed.

It is in this area of interaction where the assessor needs to understand the principles, methods, and techniques of training and knowledge/skill transfer. The assessor must be skilled enough to assess the relevance of the technique being used (i.e., games, exercises, role-playing, question and answer) as it relates to the overall training goal of the specific training event and whether such efforts were effective.

A trainer can use an exercise or technique that is known to be an enjoyable experience for those participating but that has no value in reaching the final training objective other than to build a positive feeling toward the trainer on the part of the trainees.

Since these can be used to develop a more "euphoric" sense among training participants, they can distract and inappropriately influence the assessor unless the assessor has the skills and knowledge to examine the specific segment as it relates to the training goal rather than the reaction of the trainees to the specific training segment.

Direct observation, while crucial in most trainer assessments, has several pitfalls. The first is that the observer, by his mere presence, changes the dynamics of the training situation. If there are two observers, the issue of impact on the training is even greater.

Efforts must be made to have the trainers understand that the observer is there in a nonthreatening way. Ironically, the way in which the observation is explained can often be a good initial measure of some of the trainer's skills.

In addition, if the trainees are aware this is an assessment observation and they like the trainer, the can attempt to influence the observation by performing differently than they normally would. They might participate more fully by asking questions they would not normally ask in an attempt to show the trainer as skilled. There are numerous ways in which the trainee group can modify behavior to assist the trainer. This can work against the trainer because of the group's lack of understanding of what the assessor is looking for in the assessment.

In the reverse, the trainees can attempt to harm the trainer's observation because they dislike the trainer. Whether the trainees like or dislike the trainer is not necessarily related to the knowledge transfer, the quality of the training, and/or the skills of the trainer.

Observing a training event does not mean simply watching. Critical requirements must be met in those observations:

- What type of training is being assessed?
- Which aspects of the training needs to be assessed?
- What are the objectives of the training?

- What standards will the observation be assessed against?
- What methods and techniques are being used and why?
- Over what time frame will the observations be made?

While observation is necessary in many aspects of the assessment, it is not necessary if the assessment centers on the design of training modules, aids, and so on, except as the use of the module relates to its effectiveness in the training environment. Designing of a training module or program can be assessed in a number of ways that do not require observation. Depending on the knowledge or skill being transferred through the training, design can often be measured by results. If, for example, a training module for meter readers is designed and used, and at the end of the training 100 percent of the trainees have met the goals of the training of reading "x" number of meters in "y" amount of time with 100 percent accuracy, then the training design was successful. Obviously, when a specific skill is the goal of the training, the more concrete the skill, the easier the ability to measure. The issues become more confusing when the areas of training involve less concrete skill and knowledge areas such as supervisory skills.

The what of trainer assessment requires that the assessor know specifically what he is attempting to assess. This needs to involve the trainer in the process. For example, in issues of design, it is important for the assessor to understand what the goal of the trainer was in developing the training module. It is also important to know the goals of the trainer in using various techniques within the training and to have that information before any observation because it may be that the trainer achieves his goal with the training, but it fails to achieve the ultimate corporate goal.

WHEN

This step is simply determining when specifically the assessment will occur and involves two key elements. The first is to meet with the trainer to discuss the way in which the assessment will be conducted. This initial meeting should not be loosely scheduled. Ample time should be allocated to discuss the timing and nature of the actual assessment. This initial meeting should be scheduled when the trainer is not actively dealing with an ongoing training event. Too often, the initial discussion with the trainer about the assessment occurs during a break in the training session the trainer is conducting. This is simply not the way to achieve success in the assessment. Second, the assessor and the trainer should agree about the assessment observations and when they will occur.

As mentioned earlier, the trainer should be allowed to explain to the training group that an observer will be in attendance. Because of the many reasons discussed before, including the obvious potential impact on the training group itself, more than one observation is desired. Generally, two observations is the minimum and three the more appropriate number.

With only a single observation, a trainer could change his behavior for that particular session, but it is much harder to maintain a false change over multiple observations. This is true even when it is the same training being observed with different training groups.

Three observations are generally regarded as the optimum number. The first observation will reveal issues that need to be discussed between the assessor and the trainer, and the next two observations are needed to ensure agreed on changes have been incorporated successfully.

WHERE

This is probably the easiest of the steps in an assessment. As a general rule, all assessments should occur in the workplace. Attempting to conduct the assessment in a nonworking environment or in a staged environment will not produce results with any validity.

Perhaps the best example of this can be drawn from our discussion of the meter reading training. The training environment can successfully train the meter reader to read accurately "x" number of meters within a certain time, but the training cannot provide the meter reader with the real-life ingredients that will be encountered on the job such as difficult meter locations, threatening dogs and other animals, and antagonistic homeowners. The final analysis of skill transfer is in its application in the real working world.

Simply put, the most effective place to conduct an assessment of a trainer is in the training environment. All of the cautions raised earlier about the impact on the training class need to be considered, but there is little or no justification for an assessment outside of the actual environment in which the work being assessed is performed.

WHY

The final segment of our borrowed journalism framework is why, and this has very serious implications for assessment. *Why* is the basis for the assessment. The why involves discussion between the person conducting the assessment and the trainer about the purpose of the assessment and the interaction between the two before, during, and after the training event.

Just as it is important to know where learners are before undertaking training, how they are progressing, and whether they successfully gained the knowledge or skill at the end of the training, the same is true for the trainer.

The assessor needs to know what the trainer's objectives were before the training; how they related to the corporate objectives for the training; why he selected the various training methods; how the trainer viewed the training and whether or not he believed it was successful in reaching the original goals; and why the trainer felt the way he did. This type of discussion addresses why the trainer selected specific audiovisual aids and various interactive techniques and whether the trainer thought in retrospect that the choices were successful and why or why not. Finally, this step allows the trainer to discuss the issues he believes could improve future offerings of this training.

Even when we have identified the who, what, when, where, and why of the assessment, we are not finished because, as any journalism professional will tell you, there is generally another segment to getting a complete story or completing a quality assessment and that is *how*.

HOW

The how of assessing trainers is exactly that. We need to address the manner and methods of the assessment itself. This generally falls into three parts:

1. Observation of the trainer in action with a training group.
2. Discussion with the trainer and others, before and after the observation.
3. The use of supplementary material in an evaluation and validation process.

The first two items have been sufficiently discussed earlier, except it is important to remember that discussion with the trainer is extremely important in understanding the goals of the trainer in relationship to the ultimate corporate goals of knowledge and/or skill transfer.

The last piece of this segment needs additional discussion. As we have noted several times, the actual transfer of knowledge and/or skill as a result of a training event has a direct bearing on the assessment of a trainer. If 100 percent of the trainees in a particular training event achieve and put into practice the skill or knowledge that was the subject of the training received, then the training was successful and the trainer was effective.

For this reason, effective assessment of a trainer must include material that helps in assessing the training, the training materials, and the trainer. The most obvious of the additional information available to an assessment is the end-of-course validation material. This validation material needs to be a part of the assessment.

Just as we should not ignore the end-of-course validation data, we can conversely not rely on it as the primary documentation of effectiveness. Rarely will the end-of-course validation find a 100 percent learning result. (If it does, then the goal of the training may be set too low.) It is more likely that the results will reflect a learning curve for the group of trainees.

If the learning curve is largely on the positive side, then it indicates an effective training offering. If it is largely on the negative side, it indicates problems with the training material, the trainer, or both. It is important to note that poor end-of-course validation data might indicate poor training material, not necessarily a poor trainer.

In using any test of knowledge or skill, the further from the training event, the greater the value of the information in terms of assessing trainer effectiveness. If the follow-up validation focuses on application of the knowledge or skill in the job 12 months after the training and finds a high level of usage and understanding of the knowledge or skill, then this directly reflects on the effectiveness of the training and the trainer. The goal of the training is to have the knowledge and/or skill applied in the real working world to reach a corporate goal.

Long-term validation (generally conducted 3, 6, or 12 months after the training event) sometimes reveals that some of the primary goals of the trainer in designing the training were not successful because the trainees retained the material in a totally different way. This often results when a trainer designs a high-impact segment designed to drive home the point to the trainees, but, as later revealed, the trainees remember the special impact but the not point behind it.

When conducting follow-up validation, it is often beneficial if the same instrument used at the end of the course is used again. This allows for a comparison over time of specific issues. Unfortunately, this is not always possible.

In general, even long-term follow-up questions about the trainer are not of much value as they relate to assessment. They are more valuable than questions filled out right after the training event, but because of a lack of the critical components needed for quality assessment, there is little value in questionnaires about the trainer.

There is value in a post-training interview with the trainees by the person assessing the trainer. This can be completed with or without a questionnaire. This interview allows the assessor to understand what the learner experienced during the session as it relates to the trainer.

Chapter Twelve

Trainer Assessment Inventories

INSTRUMENTS FOR OBSERVATION

If an event or a series of events, perhaps with a number of trainers, is to be observed, the assessor must have something on which to record his observations and resulting views. Typical instruments for the supplementary validation of training have already been considered. The instruments now in question relate directly to observation of the trainer, and these should be kept to a minimum so their numbers do not make their use confusing and undesirable.

The criteria for which instruments to use depend on the type of training and what it involves. Trainers of all kinds will be involved in

- Input sessions or presentations of material.
- Discussion sessions as separate events or as integral parts of another type of event.
- The control of activities, games, exercises, and role-plays and the control of the feedback and appraisal of these events.
- Demonstrations of actual tasks or operations.

Most trainer activities will be confined to these four areas. Other activities can probably be measured using only variations of the instruments.

The assessor and producer of observational instruments must remember that the purpose of the observation is to consider the effectiveness of the processes, techniques, and methods employed by the trainer, not the content of the task, unless this is so inappropriate that it affects the training process. For example, if the information given in an input session is so out of date that the trainer loses credibility with the group and also loses control of the trainees, the content is relevant in the assessment of the trainer.

A superficial look at the observation and assessment of a trainer giv-ing a presentation, a lecture, or a talk would seem to suggest this is a simple task. However, there are many factors to assess in this area, used by every trainer for some period of his job.

PRESENTATION SKILLS

The way in which the training is received by the assessor and the learners is a matter of personal judgment perhaps weighted by

- Your learning preferences.
- Your interpersonal reaction to the behavior of the trainer.
- The charisma of the trainer.
- The level of your interest in the subject.
- The level of your needs to learn about the subject.
- The methods, novel or otherwise, of the presentation.

Because all these variants exist, a consistent approach is difficult, but it is aided by a full realization of the difficulties and subjectivity associated with assessment.

Assessment of the trainer in the input session will be a personally ac-cepted model of behavior in the form of:

1. A universally accepted model of presentation skills.
2. A consistent personal model.
3. A model or approach decreed by the culture of the organization.

In most cases, the approach is a mixture of 1 and 2, although many organizations still impose specific requirements and constraints on their presenters—the trainer or other speaker will sit/stand/be still/move, speak from a lectern, be formally dressed all the time/be casu-ally dressed.

The basic model of assessment usually includes whether the trainer has considered the many environmental requirements; used effective verbal and nonverbal behaviors; included the effective use of aids—visual, audio, video—and developed an interpersonal relationship with the learning group. As suggested above, these may all vary consid-erably with the situation, but will all be included on any occasion in some form.

ENVIRONMENTAL REQUIREMENTS

Many environmental requirements may be outside the control of the trainer, but the assessor must confirm this rather than assume nothing could have been done.

The following items could be included in assessment:

- *Room comfort.* Has the trainer taken the size of the room, the type of seating, and the temperature control into account in his planning of where the training should occur? Is the extraneous noise level sufficiently low to avoid distracting the learners? If the training is taking place in a hotel, have the background music and announcement systems been silenced? Does noise from another group distract the learners?

- *Personal comfort.* Is the space sufficient for the number of learners and the training projected? What arrangements have been made for smokers? Are refreshment and meal breaks organized and known to the trainees? Are the starting and finishing times of the training days known by the learners? Have arrangements been made to allow for travel time by learners at the end of the training event?

- *Other factors.* If there is a telephone in the training room, has it been disconnected? Have arrangements been made to ensure only emergency messages will be brought to the group? Was all the advance work done properly—correspondence, notification of training, pre-course material, all workbooks and all equipment available and checked for proper operation.

- *General.* Did the trainer have a checklist for these items or did he rely on his memory? Which was the desirable option in this situation?

PRESENTATIONAL BEHAVIORS

These relate to the actual presentation skills exhibited by the trainer and include both his verbal and nonverbal skills of presentation. Items included in the assessment observation are:

General Observable Behavior

Did the trainer exhibit nervousness at the start of or during the session? Was this nervousness excessive? Did the nervousness diminish as the session progressed? Was the session content relevant, up to date, accurate, of the level required, and sufficiently comprehensive?

Verbal Behavior

Was the voice level appropriate to the size of the room and the group? Was the vocabulary used appropriate to the learning group? Was jargon used that could not be understood? Did the trainer use excessive jargon? Did the trainer have an accent that was difficult for some learners to understand? Was the material presented in an acceptable way? Was the presentation free from too many verbal idiosyncrasies? Was humor used? Was it used effectively? Did it reinforce a point of the training or was it just a release, unrelated to the training? Could the humor used be misinterpreted and be offensive to any of the learners?

Nonverbal Behavior

Most language experts agree that:

1. People react more to what we do and how we say things than to what we actually say.
2. About 70 percent of effective communication is made through nonverbal communication rather than through verbal communication.
3. Verbal communication and nonverbal communication must be congruent, otherwise the result is misunderstanding and/or suspicion.

The trainer is very sensitive to the effects of nonverbal communication because in his exposed position everybody can easily see all his body language. A leader or member of an audience who displays unacceptable behavior may be unseen in a crowd, but the person addressing that crowd is on show to all. The trainer must not forget that he is exposed to view.

Do irritating habits—money jangling, key rattling, pencil playing, finger snapping—distract the learner from the training message? Does the trainer maintain good eye contact with the group? Is the eye contact shared throughout the group or focused on only a small number of members? Does the trainer have visual habits that are distracting—looking over the group's heads to a clock in the back of the room, looking out the window while talking? Are there any sound habits that may tempt learners to count them rather than listen to the training message—grunts, "yeahs," "ems," "ahs"? To what extent is any nervousness allowed to show in the trainer's behavior—perspiration, voice loss or cracking, rapid breathing, forgetting words?

VISUAL, AUDIO, AND VIDEO AIDS

The trainer who can succeed by talking only is very rare and requires a strong charisma. But even charisma palls after a while.

Apart from varying the presentation to encourage interest, the use of aids to speech encourages learning—if we are able to see something, we learn it more easily than by hearing it alone. Some verbal descriptions without a picture of the object itself are meaningless. As the saying goes, "A picture is worth a thousand words." The use of training aids supports the verbal messages of the trainer.

When training aids are mentioned, the usual reaction is to think of the ubiquitous overhead projector and its acetate slides and the equally well known flip chart—simple visual aids equipment and material. Simplicity should not be rejected; more trainers have succeeded in putting across their message using these two simple aids than those who have attempted to be very clever in their presentations and use a host of complicated equipment.

Overhead projector (OHP) slides can be used more adventurously than is usually the case. With a little extra preparation, a simple slide can have a great impact. It requires only the imaginative use of color, shapes, and sizes in addition to normal words. Does the trainer attempt to improve his slides in this way?

Slides are more effective if parts of them are disclosed progressively rather than showing the complete slide on the screen all the time. This can be achieved by moving a piece of paper down the slide, or by laying hinged card flaps over sections that can then be disclosed or hidden, or by using a number of part slides to build up to the complete slide by adding them on top of each other. Does the trainer stick to the traditional method of displaying information, or does he attempt to use novel methods?

Even the simple acetate roll often found fixed to overhead projectors can be used more adventurously than by simply writing on the exposed part and then rolling it on to await the next entries. The roll can be prepared in advance with a series of slides sequentially drawn on it. This is particularly useful if the series is always used and in that order, although it does hinder flexibility. A roll can tell a story with almost cinematic images as the roll is turned, perhaps accompanied by music or recorded documentary. Gimmicky? Perhaps, but these and other different approaches can support and increase the facility for learning. Does the trainer experiment or is he only willing to "do what everyone has always done"?

The flip chart is generally regarded as the trainer's universal workhorse. It is easily mobile, can be set up and used under almost any conditions, and is very flexible in its use. Sheets can be prepared before the event for progressive disclosure in a sequence or even an interrupted or modified sequence. Or they can be written on as the session progresses. Does the trainer use pre-prepared charts and posters, and if so are they readable and well prepared?

In using the flip chart, is the trainer able to find the pre-prepared sheets easily among the other pages of the pad? Are the sheets imaginatively completed yet clear and understandable? Is the writing intelligible? (If this is an issue for a trainer with poor penmanship, it can be resolved by lightly tracing the words on the sheets in advance in pencil so the trainer can see them but the training class cannot and then just following the pencil with the marker.) Are colors, shapes, and sizes used imaginatively? Are the flip chart sheets clean and attractive rather than dirty and dog-eared?

One of the common uses of the flip chart is to record during the sessions the views and comments of the participants. When recording these comments, does the trainer write clearly and put down what is said rather than what he thinks or wants said? Is the recorded information treated with respect when it has been made, or is it crumpled and thrown away in sight of the group?

Does the trainer appear to be aware of the conditions of the room in relation to the use of the flip chart? Are the letters large enough to be seen throughout the room? Does he use color variation and symbols to enhance the message?

AUDIO AIDS

Before the advent of video recording, the audiocassette recorder was the only "home recording" device available. It was used to practice interviews, talks, and so on. This device still has a place in training. The cassette recorder can be used to play short pieces of prerecorded material, including music, to support or enhance the presentation. If used, does the trainer use the cassette recorder imaginatively? Did he appear to have checked the equipment in advance to ensure it worked properly?

VIDEO/FILM AIDS

The advent of the video recorder as a quality, but relatively inexpensive training tool has had a marked impact on training, but the use of this device in training has been varied among trainers. Some trainers treat the videocassette recoder/player as if it were film, using the traditional film approach of showing the entire film and then holding a discussion. The video has allowed this pattern to be changed because the video can be stopped at any point and then picked right back up. This enhances the training options tremendously, although trainers need to be careful not to overdo the stopping and starting because they may cause antagonism among the training class.

Does the trainer use either film or video effectively and smoothly? Does it tie into the subject matter appropriately in both timing and content? Is the trainer at ease operating the equipment? Does he draw discussion from the video or film?

One critical observation that needs to be made in the assessment is the purpose of the use of the film or video. As a number of studies have revealed, dimming the lights and running a film, filmstrip, video, or other photographic device signals to the trainees a pause, an opportunity to relax and regroup. This natural tendency on the part of a large portion of trainees clearly has implications for the trainer and therefore for assessing his performance. Questions should be asked such as, Was the film used to support a specific point or was it used to introduce a major point of the training? Did the discussions about the content, whether during pauses or at the end of the video/film, show that many of the trainees did not understand the point of the video/film? Was the major point of the video/film re-addressed in the training after the video/film?

A good trainer may use videos and/or films as a pause in as well as an enhancement of the training but needs to understand the reasons for each use and the positive and negative impact of his choices.

COMPUTER-ASSISTED LEARNING

Increasingly, computer-assisted learning is becoming common in the training world. Forward-projection computer screens allow trainers to use computers much like an overhead, but with all of the computer capacity available to them. This device makes it possible to create all sorts of visual presentations limited only by the imagination of the trainer.

Even without the forward-projection computer, the computer has changed the face of training in many ways. Computer-assisted learning, especially in terms of specific skill training, allows each individual to work at his own pace and allows for constant monitoring of the learning. Skill training is perhaps the one area of training where learning can be effectively monitored through the interactive nature of the computer training.

In most cases, even with the most sophisticated computer-based training effort, an instructor is needed to supplement and assist the students. Increasingly, a large number of training events are involving some interactive computer training with more traditional training approaches. In these cases, the questions that need to be asked are: Is the instructor familiar with the training provided in the CAT (computer-assisted training)? Does the trainer monitor the feedback from each of the students regularly and adjust his support efforts accordingly? Does the instructor supplement the material within the module in appropriate ways?

GENERAL ISSUES

Can the trainer control the beginnings and endings of presentations? A bad start can ruin an otherwise effective presentation, and a bad ending can undo all the work that preceded it. Did he cover all of the material intended and was it aimed correctly at the training group?

Learning is not a continuous experience at the same level. The ability to absorb training is a cyclical thing and is greater at certain times than at others. (For instance, learning absorption is very low immediately following a heavy meal such as a luncheon.) Does the trainer consider this cyclical nature in scheduling the points with the greatest importance when the learning absorption is greatest? Does the trainer attempt to redirect his material to accommodate cyclical patterns as they become obvious?

ASSESSMENT INVENTORIES

A suggested inventory when assessing a presentation is given in Appendix One. This is the first in a small series presented here that can be used within any organization by modifying the entries according to the situation and the assessment needs. A set of guidelines is also included at the start of the assessment guide, but not repeated for each guide for space reasons.

This type of inventory can be used in a variety of ways, and assessors will, through experimentation, find the way that suits them best. Whichever approach is used, assessors will find it useful to:

1. Familiarize themselves fully before the event with all the assessment aspects included (a checklist is included with the inventory).

2. Use the inventory during the event rather than rely on memory. To what extent the inventory is completed during the event depends on the assessor's approach. Some find it convenient to make entries in the comments spaces only, leaving the ratings to be completed afterward; others rate the items during the event and add comments at their leisure later; and yet others use only the checklist with free notes and complete the full inventory after the event.

The types of variation possible within the instruments shown in the appendices include principally content and rating scales. The content varies according to the type of event and the specific needs of the assessor. Assessment can be approached from a positive or a negative viewpoint, and although positive approaches are more satisfactory psychologically, they are often more difficult to assess. For example, in Appendix One, the first question relates to the nervousness of the presenter at the start of the presentation. The positive viewpoint would suggest looking at his confidence shown at the start of the presentation, rather than his nervousness. The decision about which approach to take must rest with the assessor. I find it much easier when assessing to look for the failings initially—these are usually much more evident than the successes. If failings are being looked for, but they are not evident, then the other end of the scale reflects the positive viewpoint that success is there rather than failure.

How would I recognize confidence? When we say we are looking for signs of confidence, most observers rate a presenter as confident usually "because they do not exhibit signs of nervousness." But this depends on whether the assessor is perfectly clear about what he is looking for.

The rating scales in the appendices have five scoring divisions. I am usually best able to work with seven. Many assessors, however, find that seven levels of skill is too many to cope with, but they find five levels acceptable. Others find that even five levels are too difficult or not realistic; consequently, they prefer a three-scale rating approach.

Similarly, many people find it difficult to accept an odd number in rating scales—5 or 7—because they believe others treat the 3 or 4 score as average. Consequently, they prefer a 4 or 6 scale. Use the one with which you feel most comfortable. The principal criterion is that scoring on whatever scale must be as meaningful as possible.

Another area linked with the first variation discussed above relates to the apparent or real subjectivity of the "measure." An example of this is sincerity. Some people argue that because sincerity is an emotion or feeling, it cannot really be observed and assessed and therefore should not appear in an assessment instrument. If the assessor believes he cannot recognize apparent sincerity, then it should be excluded.

Many aspects of assessment fall into the subjective category. We must be aware of interpreting the behavior of the trainer being assessed. All we can go on is the observable behavior; anything else is dangerous. If I am listening to and watching a trainer present a session, I may have a feeling whether or not that trainer is being sincere. This is based on whether his behavior appears to me that he is being sincere in the things he is saying or doing. It doesn't matter whether he is sincere or not—as long as his overt behavior appears consistently sincere to me. Some observers may not be able to recognize overt sincere or insincere behavior. If this is so and they recognize this inability (and they may be being more honest about their abilities than those of us who claim to be able to recognize a sincere behavior), then this category of assessment must be excluded.

Whichever method is used, the assessor will usually make notes during the event. Although this must be performed openly, it must not be too apparent, otherwise the trainer's performance might be affected. The main problem encountered by assessors in using these inventories is in determining the standards for the ratings.

DISCUSSION-LEADING SKILLS ASSESSMENT

Assessment of the trainer's discussion-leading skills is necessary when he leads discussions, either as separate events in a training program or as integral parts of an input session. Whichever discussion activity is being considered, the techniques are the same and show standard leader behavior for this activity.

The main role for the trainer in discussions with the learners is initiator and then controller of the discussion, rarely the principal contributor to the event. Did the trainer lead the discussion or did he take it over? How was the discussion introduced? How was the event handled if the discussion emerged naturally? Were the learners clear about what they were to discuss? Were the objectives of the discussion made clear to the learners?

If the discussion is to be a significant event in its own right, rather than part of another event, the initiating trainer has to prepare for the discussion in the same way he prepared for an input session. Was the trainer's approach clear and determined? Had the trainer a shopping list or agenda for the discussion? How obvious was the use of aids? Did the trainer start the discussion with a visual/audio aid? Had the trainer prepared questions to inject if the discussion ran out of steam?

During the discussion, the trainer asks questions and listens carefully to the discussion. What kinds of questions did the trainer pose? Were they appropriate? Did they help or hinder the discussion? Did the trainer show he was listening to the learners' contributions? How did he demonstrate this?

The third role of the trainer is to end the discussion or see that it is ended in a clear and positive manner, and that the objective has been achieved and necessary action agreed to. To what extent were summaries used during the discussion? Was there a comprehensive summary at the end of the discussion? Who was responsible for making the summaries? Were the summaries always clear and comprehensive, and to what extent did the trainer ensure this was so? To what extent were the learners allowed/encouraged to express their satisfaction or displeasure with the discussion? Was the discussion controlled so it was contained within the time allocated?

The assessor will be aware that a discrete discussion session is to occur and be observed; that there is the intention to include a discussion within a specific input session; or that during an input session a discussion is likely to start. He will ensure that he has an appropriate observation instrument, particularly in the last case. A suggested discussion-leading observation inventory is shown in Appendix Two.

ACTIVITIES, GAMES, EXERCISES, ROLE-PLAYS

Many training events include a number of practical activities, which may be games designed for specific skill purposes—decision making, problem solving, negotiation—and people care games such as action mazes.

Activities may take the form of syndicate or group exercises in which learners take on roles, solve problems as a group, exhibit effective group behavior, and so on. Role-plays are either of imaginary or real-life situations, and these may be observed by the trainer and colleagues, either directly, through closed-circuit TV, or on video. The role events may also occur as "hot" role-play that arises naturally during the discussion/activity of a real-life problem. This can be developed into an immediate role-play with the initiators of the situation "living" the situation. If the problem is one that has been brought to the training by one of the learners, the originator of the problem may play himself or the person with whom he is in conflict or even both parties, as in the "empty chair" approach.

Whatever the practical event might be, there are likely to be common factors. The activity must be introduced, briefings must be given either orally or from written instructions, and all the arrangements made for the activity to proceed. During the activity, the trainer observes the process, usually with little or no intervention. After the event, the participants, the arranged observers, and the trainer discuss what happened, the process, the behaviors, and the results and give feedback from their different viewpoints. (A discussion between the trainer and assessor after the event about the activity would be appropriate.)

In activities of this nature, the trainer might play one or more of a number of roles. But the event has to be initiated. Did the trainer present the activity clearly? Did the trainer ensure that participants were clear about what was expected of them? Were written/oral briefs clear and comprehensive but constrained in extent and complexity? Was it made clear how much time was allocated to the event? If leaders were appointed, did they know who their group members were, and did the group members know who their leader was? Were clear location instructions given? Were syndicate or subgroup activity rooms prepared?

During the activity, the trainer's role can be that of interventionist or the deliberate noninterventionist. The former can interrupt the group when he sees it going along a path that will lead to failure, not bringing out the lessons he wants to emerge, or taking too much time on a nonessential part. There is always the likelihood that the group members will

- Accept the lead and do only what is obviously expected of them.
- Reject the lead and go ahead as they want to.
- Reject the lead and come into conflict with the trainer.
- Accept the help gratefully.

The problem in all these reactions, even the last one, is that much of the resulting activity is dictated by the trainer and consequently the learning by the group may be minimal or nonexistent.

The alternative approach is when the trainer withdraws from active participation, having started the activity, and deliberately does not intervene whatever the provocation. There must be total nonintervention. However much the group might appeal to the trainer for help or when he sees problems arising within the group, he must resist the temptation. Of course, if the safety of the group is involved, then he must intervene, but the intervention must be a last resort. Part of a group's real learning occurs when members find, because of a decision they have made, they have gone wrong and have to make further decisions to solve the problem. What kind of strategy does the trainer adopt? How well does he stick to it? How appropriate is the strategy for the situation? Does he intervene at appropriate times? Even though he has a nonintervention strategy, does he intervene when it is essential for him to do so?

As important as the activity itself is the post-activity discussion intended to extract all the learning points that emerged during the activity. The format of this discussion depends on the type of activity. After an exercise or game, the feedback is often given mainly by observers who have been briefed to look at certain parts of the activity process and structure and the behavior of the participants, particularly the appointed leader. In addition, the feelings and reactions of the participants can be sought. Finally, the trainer can make a contribution if there is anything left to say, certainly in picking up the pieces and preparing the participants for the next activity.

In role-plays, the trainer is also responsible for controlling the feedback and appraisal, taking an active part only if significant aspects or learning points have been missed or to present an alternative viewpoint. Otherwise the trainer will probably leave the main appraisal in, say, a face-to-face interview role-play, to the interviewer and the interviewee with support from the observers.

Did the trainer explain the appraisal/feedback system clearly? Did the trainer encourage the participants and the observers to take the feedback roles? To what extent did the trainer contribute to the appraisal? Was this contribution relevant and appropriate? To what extent did the trainer take over the appraisal? How necessary was this?

In addition to these issues, other questions need to be considered in the evaluation. Did the trainer allow an ineffective or inaccurate feedback to go unchallenged? How was the challenge raised? Was closed-circuit TV or video recording used? Was it used effectively? Was it drawn in to the feedback portion to offer visual examples?

An example of an observational inventory for this type of trainer and training event is shown in Appendix Three.

DEMONSTRATIONS

A common procedure, particularly in mechanical, technical, and procedural training, is for the real object, device, or system to be used during the training. In such cases, the object needs to be described and demonstrated and opportunities given for learners to have hands-on practice and experience with the object. Such a demonstration must be performed in an interesting and effective way or else an important opportunity for a live training experience is lost. The *demonstration* includes not only description, display, and demonstration of the object by the trainer, but also the opportunity for the learners to demonstrate their learned ability.

Has the trainer made examples of the subject available? Is there opportunity for hands-on practice by the learner? Does the trainer ensure that everybody has an opportunity to practice? Does the trainer ensure that the learners really understand what they are doing and why?

An observation inventory suitable for this kind of event is given in Appendix Four.

OTHER OBSERVATIONS

The four inventories described above do not exhaust the types of observational instruments available. Earlier, behavior analysis was described as a very suitable instrument for observing, recording, and analyzing behavior. This is used mainly with training groups, but a behavior analysis form can easily be constructed to be used in observing specific behaviors by the trainer in a number of situations. Other activity analysis forms, similar to behavior analysis but concentrating on the use of structure, can be developed for special occasions. Most trainer observation assessment purposes normally are covered by one or more of the four inventories described, either in the form shown in the appendices or modified to suit the particular occasion.

Some assessors prefer a combined inventory when a training session being observed includes, for example, a lecture with a discussion and a role-play. The three inventories can be used, but Appendix Five shows how the assessment items can be combined into one document. Activities common to the three parts of the session have been identified, followed by questions specific to the parts of the session. The guides can be combined in other ways depending on the type of inventory required.

TRAINEE ASSESSMENT

The approach with the highest risk factor and the potentially lowest realistic result is to ask the learners to complete an end-of-course assessment of the trainer in addition to the usual end-of-course assessment of the training. The "euphoric" factor has already been mentioned as well as the large number of cautions resulting from the lack of knowledge of training techniques and deep personal involvement in the training. However, the learners have been directly on the receiving end of the trainer's actions and relationship with them and although they may not be in the best position to comment, some realism might emerge even out of emotive statements. So asking them to complete an assessment is not a complete waste and may produce useful results.

If it is obvious that there has been a high degree of euphoria, the assessor must look carefully to see whether the trainees are reacting only to a charismatic trainer. If the mood is depressive, what has gone wrong? To what extent has the trainer or his potential lack of skills contributed to or caused this? The answer can be found by using the learners' comments in parallel with the observations of the assessor and others. This suggests the most appropriate occasion on which to seek learner assessments is when other observations are being made—it is dangerous to use the trainee assessments alone. The comments of the learners are principally at the reactive rather than the considered level. The learners are applying immediate reaction rather than a delayed consideration based on learning needs, methods, techniques, and styles.

Many trainers have had learners leave the course dissatisfied, yet on meeting them later, they have admitted they learned a great deal. Time and consideration has shown them that what happened was essential to the learning process.

If the learners are asked to make a trainer assessment, any request must be short and simple, particularly if they are also being asked to complete a training validation questionnaire. The trainer assessment questionnaire must be introduced carefully and openly, giving the learners every opportunity for anonymity.

The format in Appendix Six is a suggested one that can be modified easily depending on the circumstances and in conjunction with the assessor's approach.

The observation and assessment guides reproduced in the appendices do not guarantee that assessment is made easy, nor that common standards will result, but they go a long way toward achieving these aims by providing consistent means of observing and recording. The differences between the people who might assess—their personal values and skills in judgment—means 100 percent consistency is never possible. But if the formats suggested are used, the differences can be demonstrated and discussed.

Chapter Thirteen

Costs and Plans

If observation inventories of the types described in the previous chapter are used to assess a trainer in action, and this assessment shows the trainer is effective and the training is valid, the employing organization can be reasonably sure it is receiving value for its money. The assessment of the monetary value of training and trainers can be as subjective and as difficult as the validation of some of the forms of training previously mentioned. If attempts are made to extend this cost or value analysis to include monetary levels in the overall evaluation, the difficulties become even more evident.

Cost value analysis must be part of the assessment of a trainer once his actual training abilities have been confirmed, otherwise the organization will have no idea, for example, how many trainers it must employ to perform the training desired. How much is a trainer worth? What is the total net cost of the training to the organization? What is the cost of a training day? How many trainers/training days can the organization afford?

To assess these values, the assessor must be able to attribute a cost to everything connected with the training. This is easier said than done!

THE COSTS OF TRAINING

The costs attributable to the training function can be divided into three main sections:

1. Fixed costs relating to the training establishment.
2. Supportive costs in terms of trainers, and learners.
3. Opportunity costs.

Fixed Costs

Fixed costs include those that are reasonably regular and fixed over a period of time, such as one year. They can comprise:

1. Salaries and fringe benefits for training and administrative staff in the training department as well as costs for guest lecturers and consultants.
2. Costs of the training facility including capital equipment and maintenance, office space for training personnel and training rooms.
3. Utility costs attributable to the training function.

Supportive Costs

Costs incurred for trainers and learners are called support costs. They occur less frequently than fixed costs and can include:

1. External costs for training and the trainers at an off-property site such as hotel or conference center including room rental charges for meeting space, equipment charges for the meeting room, and room and board for the trainers.
2. Travel and out-of-pocket expenses for the trainers.
3. Equipment, books, and material and any associated expenses.
4. Room and board for the learners.
5. Travel and out-of-pocket expenses for the learners.
6. The learners' salaries.

Opportunity Costs

Although learners' salaries are paid while the learner is in the training course, the learners are not directly contributing to company output. The value of this noncontribution is often described as the opportunity cost— the value of that individual's services if he had been contributing directly in his job to the company output. In many ways, this has to be a subjective amount, although some companies claim they are able to calculate this lost opportunity value accurately.

EVALUATION

Even more subjective are any attempts to link the overall value of an individual's training and development to an increase in work output, efficiency, higher earning value, and so on. It is very difficult, if not impossible, to attribute a value to the total learning process. Few attempts have been made, and these were little more than intelligent guesses. Trained people who are involved in direct operation tasks can have their efficiency assessed and, if they were unskilled before the training, any increase in skill and output value resulting can be attributed to the training. In most training cases, this is not possible. The problem is so great that organizations attempting to assess the cost of training simply ignore this factor. If it is consistently ignored, comparisons can be made between one period and another, but it must be accepted that a portion of the function is being ignored.

COST ANALYSIS

Using the figures related to the costs summarized above, a company can produce a monetary statement from which a number of conclusions can be drawn—the cost of the training function; cost of the training function per individual; cost of the training function per learner; and so forth. These are useful within the constraints mentioned above. The main advantage I have found has been in comparing them from one period to another. It does not matter much if the figures are not completely accurate representations, provided the same calculation and methods of calculations are used on each occasion.

In the simplest analysis, a unit cost of training per trainer can be obtained by adding all the known costs—fixed, support, and opportunity. If this figure is divided by the number of people who contribute toward the training—the training manager, trainers, administrative training staff, and external speakers and consultants—the resulting figure is one form of cost. For example, if the sum of all the costs is $400,000 per year with a training staff of eight, the unit cost per trainer is $50,000. This calculation masks a number of factors—cost of external training and open learning, high course numbers, and a value based on the evaluation of the training and transfer to work. Even without these other factors, it at least gives a baseline measure that can be used as a comparative costing from one year to another, using the same set of factors.

Say the following year, the total costs of the same factors had risen to $480,000, the cost per trainer would have increased to $60,000, a 20 percent increase. There may be a good explanation for this rise if an inquiry is made.

Costing can be approached from another angle. If the total training cost were $400,000 annually and 3,000 learners passed through 200 course programs during that year, then the cost per learner was $133 and the cost per course was $2,000. If the following year, the costs rose to $480,000 but the number of learners increased to 4,500 and the number of courses to 300, then the cost per learner was $107 and $1,600 per course, in both cases a decrease over prior year costs within an increase in total expenses.

It is also possible to cost the training in terms of the number of learners who have attended the events. One method to reduce your per course costs is to increase the number of learners. The trainer salary and all the fixed costs remain constant, and the only increases are small ones in terms of the additional learners and their salaries. This is a very common practice when outside consultants are used because the costs for the consultant are fixed regardless of the numbers of learners in most cases.

However, by increasing the numbers, you must be careful that you are not harming the quality of the training. Every format has a point beyond which additional people begin to take away from the learning opportunities rather than add to them.

The examples quoted above are all basic approaches to costing without considering the many plus and minus factors, if an attempt is being made to balance the value of the training to the organization with increased business and hence profits. It is almost impossible, except in the simplest of cases, to be sure that any improvement in performance is due to the training.

These problems must be recognized and care taken not to base too many decisions on costs alone.

PLANNING FOR ASSESSMENT

By this stage in my description of how to approach the assessment of the effectiveness of trainers, the potential assessor will be starting to consider the trainer he has to assess. Factors to be considered include:

- Where do the trainer's preferences lie?
- Do they show?
- How flexible is the trainer between types?
- What type of training approach and attitude does the organization require?

- How flexible or capable of being influenced is the organization?
- What type of training has to be performed?
- Can the training format be modified?
- What needs to be assessed?
- Which is the most effective means of assessment in this case?
- What other approaches can be used in support?
- To what extent should other supportive approaches be used?
- How much assessment has to be done?
- Which inventories are available?
- Which inventories are the most suitable?

This can be a bewildering set of choices, but decisions must be made. These decisions will be eased if there is a plan to follow. The plan proposed here has been followed in recent years by a number of organizations that saw the need to have an assessment system for their trainers and to plan the process to maximize assessor resources, minimize resource time, and maximize effectiveness.

PLANNING FLOWCHART

Some organizations have modified the plans to suit their particular requirements; others have followed the full plan summarized in the flowchart in Figure 13–1.

Several of the stages on the flowchart require comments. The remainder have all been adequately covered in earlier text.

Stage 1

Figure 13–1 shows that one of the early decisions to be made concerns who is responsible for making the assessments. The options available are:

1. An external examining body.
2. An experienced and qualified external assessor.
3. The immediate supervisor of the trainer(s).
4. A specially selected assessment group.

This group would be drawn from within the company from individuals who have the necessary skills; who have some of the necessary skills and who can, with training, supplement these skills; who might benefit

FIGURE 13–1
Planning Flowchart

Training Skills Assessment Plan for Trainers

---

1. Who is to assess?
2. Who is to be assessed?
3. What time is required and available?
4. When (over what period) is the assessment to occur?
5. Where is the assessment to be undertaken?
6. Produce a statement of intent?
   a. Obtain/provide comprehensive job description
   (forward plan)
   b. Correlate job description with competency
   standards (or standards expected)
   c. Obtain from organization any specific corporate demands
7. Meet trainers for initial discussion
   a. Discussion of assessment plan
   b. Confirmation by training manager and trainer of use of appropriate training
   modes
8. Discuss and agree to mutual expectations and arrangements
   a. Pre-training discussion
   b. Observation of training events
   c. Post-training discussion
9. Discuss and agree on optional additional assessments
   a. Parallel self-assessment
   b. Parallel peer assessment
   c. Parallel trainee assessment
10. Take agreed assessment action as in 8 and 9 above
11. Additional supportive analyses
    a. Analyze training validations
    b. Make evaluation approaches or ensure availability of any evaluation results
    c. Make evaluation visits or ensure availability of any visit results
12. Complete assessment reports and overall assessment report in format decided
    a. Interim reports on individual assessments
    b. Overall report at end of assessment

---

from taking on this part-time work as part of their career development; or simply those who have been identified as having, following training, the potential as assessors. The actions necessary to bring them up to an effective level in assessment depend on which category the individual comes from. A training expense is almost certain to be incurred, but this is an initial expense only and provides a group of trained assessors.

Stage 6

At this stage in the planning process, the statements to be produced are concerned with a description of what the trainer should be doing, how he should be doing it, and so on, from both the viewpoints of effective training and any demands imposed by the organization. As in any form of appraisal or assessment, the necessary starting point is identifying what is required. Otherwise the question is raised, "Effectiveness against what standards?" It is here that the existence of a comprehensive job description is essential. This must be more than cosmetic and must include as much detail as possible for the use in the assessment. This is the basis against which the assessment is made. If the description is incomplete, the assessment will be incomplete.

Stage 10

It is difficult to lay down rules for how much assessment of an individual should be made. Much depends on the individual and the assessments made after the start of the process. If the first assessment observation of the trainer in a lecture session suggests he is an excellent presenter, the temptation is to accept that and require no further observation. Restricting observation is risky for a number of reasons. One of these is that the session observed may have been a specialty subject of that trainer. If he were to be observed presenting a different type of session, the assessment might not be as good. Even with good trainers, a minimum of two observations is essential.

If the first observation suggests a number of areas for improvement, these are naturally discussed in the post-observation discussion with the trainer, and arrangements are made for improvement. The trainer then needs to be observed again, following action to make the improvements.

If a trainer includes input sessions, discussion sessions, activity sessions, and demonstrations in a training event, it is necessary for all these to be assessed to produce a final, complete assessment. This is the ideal, because it can represent a considerable investment of time in the observations alone, without any allied meetings and discussions. In practice, therefore, the ideal may not be met but it is something to be aimed for.

Stages 11a, 11b, and 11c

Stage 11*a* is usually the examination by the assessor of the end-of-course validation inventories completed by the trainees that concentrate principally on the training, although this can be an excellent indicator of the trainer's skills. There is usually no need to examine and analyze every questionnaire for every course. A 20 percent selection should give sufficient indication that all seems to be well or that problems exist either due to the training or the trainer or both. Again, the analysis can be extended beyond the 20 percent if that level does not give all the information necessary.

Stage 11*b* must occur after the direct observation period and is linked with the 3-, 6-, or 12-month evaluation action taken by the trainers with the learners and their immediate supervisors. If this evaluation is performed by follow-up inventories, the assessor needs to analyze a percentage of those responses in the same way as the end-of-the course inventories.

Stage 11*c* is ordinarily a luxury but might become more important in the assessment if the inventories in stage 11*b* suggest all is not well. It may then be necessary for the assessor to interview the learners and their supervisors in their workplace to determine the full extent of the problem.

Stage 12

Recording action taken and the results is a useful part of the assessment exercise and is essential in organizations that require a full written report from the assessor. A ring binder may be useful as a logbook in which to file the documents used in the assessment—the updated, working document, job description, and competence standards (if any); any descriptive material produced by the assessor about the trainer resulting from his discussions with the trainer and others before the assessment; documents relating to the training to be assessed, and in particular statements of objectives and methods; completed inventories relating to the observations made by the assessor, trainer's peer, and trainees; records of the postobservation discussions with agreements for action; analyses of end-of-course validations; and any evaluation measures attempted.

This logbook can then become a permanent record of that trainer for personnel use and as supportive material in the organization's appraisal system.

CONCLUSIONS

The warning comments at the end of Chapter 12 relating to the use of observational instruments can also be applied to the use of plans for assessment. Complete success cannot be assured by the availability of a plan, however well conceived and executed, but it should enhance the likelihood of success as opposed to an indiscriminate attempt at assessment. Even if things go wrong, it is usually easier to modify a plan to fit the changed circumstances than immediately to decide on action under duress. The plan may not fully succeed, but at least it will be possible to identify the failure and establish its cause.

Trainer Assessment-Guide

The purpose of the individual sections in each trainer assessment guide, Appendices One to Five, is to offer a rating scale and, perhaps more importantly, space to make comments about why that rating was given. The rating scale used is a scale of 1 to 5, but this can be varied according to personal preferences—an even-number scale 1 to 4 or 6, or an odd-number scale 1 to 5 or 7.

Appendix Five is a combined guide for a session that includes a lecture, a discussion, and an activity. The most common observations have been combined and separate sections provided for each part of the session. Any of the sessions can be combined in this way as required.

Appendix Five is for use by learners to give information about their views of the skills of the trainer.

The guidance for use notes are included here once only. However, they should precede each individual observational assessment guide.

GUIDANCE FOR USE

1. Familiarize yourself with the objectives of the session and discuss these with the trainer involved. Not every item in the notes will be used by every trainer on every occasion. You should concentrate on the appropriate ones.

2. Familiarize yourself with the subject headings in this assessment and be prepared to observe and note all those relevant.

3. Enter the rating numbers wherever you can, but remember that many of the behaviors will change during the session and you will need to make an overall assessment. For example, you can rate immediately the section on "Opening," but you will have to wait until later to rate the "Continuation" section.

4. Circle the rating you believe reflects most closely the trainer's behavior and performance. Take account only of what you

observe. A rating of 4 does not equate to any hypothetical average; it represents a scoring level between 3 and 5. If a word has to be associated with 4, this could be *satisfactory*.

5. During the session, take rough notes in order to enter final comments in the relevant spaces of the assessment guide. Again take account only of what you actually observe.

6. At all times try to be as objective as possible in your assessments, even though some of the assessments are subjective. Only assess what you observe, that is the overt behavior of the person being assessed.

7. Use the spaces after each scoring scale as fully as possible to record your comments. Usually comments will be necessary only when the rating is less than good, but the spaces should also be used to mention particularly useful or effective techniques.

PRACTICAL APPLICATIONS

Whichever turns out to be the most effective—the Trainer Task Inventory described earlier, or the competence standards—one painful fact will have become apparent. There is no approach that does not involve a complex and perhaps exceptionally long listing of factors to be considered. This is particularly so when we consider a varied type of occupation such as that of a trainer—of whatever ilk—and an assessment is made of the degree of complexity. If the tasks and roles are simplified to too great an extent, there may be little value in the end result. If the list of items to be assessed is too long, the instrument may not be used because of the inherent difficulties. Compromises would seem to be available, but in this field this may be more ineffective than the extremes.

Much may depend on the way the inventory is to be used. If it is to be simply a catalog of tasks that, once completed, requires only occasional updating and modification, an extensive listing may be acceptable. However, if a working instrument with constant reference is necessary, a different format of guidelines must be introduced. What is encouraging is that attention is now being taken of analyses that, with assessment, can be utilized in many ways—recruitment, appraisal, selection, assessment for job and qualification, job description, and so on. Although the task may appear monumental, once produced, and provided the will to maintain it is there, a long-lasting instrument will be available.

Lecture Sessions

Checklist

1. Opening platform presence
2. Opening of session
3. Continuation of session
4. Eye contact (showing interest)
5. Sincerity
6. Enthusiasm
7. General manner
8. Voice
9. Visual aids
10. Visual aids relevance
11. Visual aids quality
12. Visual aids use
13. Subject coverage
14. Use of session notes
15. Use of questions
16. Response to questions
17. Learner involvement
18. Classroom control
19. Handouts—adequacy
20. Handouts 2—relevance
21. Closing the session
22. Timing
23. Pace
24. Appropriate approach

25. Creativity
26. Overall rating
27. Any other comments

Trainer Assessment Guide

Lecture sessions

1. *Opening platform presence*
   To what extent did the trainer exhibit nervousness during the opening stages?

   None   1   2   3   4   5   Greatly
   How?

   How did it disappear as the session continued?
   Quickly   1   2   3   4   5   Not at all

2. *Opening of session*
   To what extent did the speaker obtain attention from the start?
   Greatly   1   2   3   4   5   Little
   How?

3. *Continuation of the sessions*
   To what extent did the speaker maintain attention as the session progressed?
   All the time   1   2   3   4   5   Lost it
   How?

4. *Eye contact (showing interest)*
   To what extent did the speaker maintain eye contact with the group?
   When speaking
   Most of the time   1   2   3   4   5   Rarely
   In what way?

   When listening
   Most of time   1   2   3   4   5   Rarely
   In what way?

5. *Sincerity*
   How sincere and committed to the subject did the speaker appear to be?
   Very   1   2   3   4   5   Not at all
   How did this show?

6. *Enthusiasm*
How enthusiastic was the speaker's manner?
Very   1   2   3   4   5   Not at all
How was this evidenced?

7. *General manner*
To what extent did the speaker's manner relax you and encourage you to listen?
A great deal   1   2   3   4   5   Little
What distracting mannerisms were present?

8. *Voice*
How clear to the whole group was the speaker?
Very clear   1   2   3   4   5   Unclear
If unclear or tending toward unclear, in what way?

How appropriate was the language used?
Appropriate   1   2   3   4   5   Inappropriate
If inappropriate or tending toward inappropriate, in what way?

9. *Visual aid*
To what extent did the speaker use visual aids to vary the presentation?
A great deal   1   2   3   4   5   None

10. *Visual and relevancy*
How relevant to the training were the visual aids?
Relevant   1   2   3   4   5   Not relevant
In what way?

11. *Visual aids quality*
What was the quality of the visual aids used?
Excellent   1   2   3   4   5   Poor
Why?

12. *Visual aids use*
How effectively were the visual aids used?
Very well   1   2   3   4   5   Badly
How?

13. *Subject coverage*
How well within the objectives was the subject covered?
Completely   1   2   3   4   5   Poorly
What was omitted or unclear?

14. *Use of session notes*
Was the use of session notes distracting?

Not at all   1   2   3   4   5   Very much
In what way?

15. *Use of questions*
How well did the speaker use questions to the group?
Very well   1   2   3   4   5   Badly
How?

16. *Response to questions*
How well did the speaker respond to questions from the group?
Very well   1   2   3   4   5   Badly
How?

17. *Learner involvement*
To what extent were the learners involved in the session?
A great deal   1   2   3   4   5   Not at all
How appropriate was this level?

18. *Classroom control*
How well did the teacher control the session and the learners?
Effectively   1   2   3   4   5   Ineffectively
In what way?

19. *Handouts*
How adequate were the handouts?
Adequate   1   2   3   4   5   Inadequate
How?

20. *Handouts 2*
How relevant were the handouts?
Relevant   1   2   3   4   5   Not relevant
Why?

21. *Closing the session*
How well did the speaker bring the session to a close?
Well   1   2   3   4   5   Badly
What was the cause of this?
Was a final summary used?

22. *Timing*
How well did the speaker keep within the time constraints?
Completely   1   2   3   4   5   Badly
What were the principal causes?

23. *Pace*
How well did the trainer pace the presentation?
Very well   1   2   3   4   5   Badly
How?

24. *Appropriate approach*
    Was this the most appropriate tactical approach for this subject or group?
    If not, what approach might be more appropriate?

25. *Creativity*
    To what extent was creativity of approach, methods, resources, practiced as required?
    Fully   1   2   3   4   5   Not at all
    In what circumstances?

26. *Overall rating*
    How would you rate the presentation of the session overall?
    Excellent   1   2   3   4   5   Poor

27. *Any other comments*

Discussion Leading

Checklist

1. Opening platform presence
2. Opening of session
3. Sincerity
4. Enthusiasm
5. Setting the scene
6. Introducing the topic
7. Visual aids
8. Visual aids relevancy
9. Visual aids quality
10. Visual aids use
11. Discussion notes
12. Use of discussion notes
13. Use of questions
14. Types of question
15. Response to questions
16. Listening
17. Interventions
18. Value of interventions
19. Use of group
20. Bringing-in
21. Dealing with various members
22. Closing the session
23. Timing
24. Appropriate approach

25. Overall rating
26. Any other comments

Trainer Assessment Guide

Discussion Leading

1. *Opening platform presence*
   To what extent did the trainer exhibit nervousness during the opening stages?
   None 1 2 3 4 5 Greatly
   How:

   How did it disappear as the session continued?
   Quickly 1 2 3 4 5 Not at all

2. *Opening of session*
   To what extent did the speaker obtain attention from the start?
   Greatly 1 2 3 4 5 Little
   How?

3. *Sincerity*
   How sincere and committed to the subject did the speaker appear to be?
   Very 1 2 3 4 5 Not at all
   What behaviors occurred?

4. *Enthusiasm*
   How enthusiastic was the speaker's manner?
   Very 1 2 3 4 5 Not at all
   In what way?

5. *Setting the scene*
   To what extent did the trainer prepare the discussion area before the start of the discussion?
   Well 1 2 3 4 5 Not at all

6. *Introducing the topic*
   How well did the trainer introduce the topic for discussion?
   Clearly 1 2 3 4 5 In a confused manner
   What happened?

7. *Visual aids*
   To what extent did the speaker use visual aids to vary the presentation?
   A great deal 1 2 3 4 5 None

8. *Visual aid relevancy*
   To what extent were the visual aids, if used, relevant to the situation?
   Very   1   2   3   4   5   Not at all
   In what way?

9. *Visual aids quality*
   What was the quality of the visual aids used?
   Excellent   1   2   3   4   5   Poor
   How?

10. *Visual aids use*
    How effectively were the visual aids used?
    Very well   1   2   3   4   5   Badly
    How?

11. *Discussion notes*
    Did the trainer have a prepared discussion note sheet/shopping list?
    Yes/no

12. *Use of discussion notes*
    If the trainer had discussion notes, how well were they used?
    Unobtrusively   1   2   3   4   5   Obtrusively
    In what way?

13. *Use of questions*
    How well did the leader use questions to the group?
    Very well   1   2   3   4   5   Badly
    In what way?

14. *Types of questions*
    Which types of questions did the leader use more than others? (place in descending order of use as far as possible)

Open	*Closed*
Multiple	Hypothetical
Leading	Aggressive
Multiple choice	Reflective
Testing understanding	Others

15. *Response to questions*
    How well did the speaker respond to questions from the group?

Very well   1   2   3   4   5   Badly
How?

16. *Listening*
    To what extent did the leader appear to listen when the group
    members were talking?
    Fully   1   2   3   4   5   Not at all
    What were the indications of this degree of listening?

17. *Interventions*
    To what extent did the leader intervene in the discussion?
    Rarely   1   2   3   4   5   Often

18. *Value of interventions*
    When the leader intervened, were these interventions
    Appropriate   1   2   3   4   5   Inappropriate
    What types of interventions were used?

19. *Use of group*
    To what extent did the leader bring in the quiet members?
    A great deal   1   2   3   4   5   Not at all
    What happened?

20. *Bringing-in*
    How did the leader bring in the quiet members?
    With skill   1   2   3   4   5   Clumsily
    What happened?

21. *Dealing with various members*
    How well did the leader deal with difficult members?
    Well   1   2   3   4   5   Badly
    With what results?

22. *Closing the discussion*
    How well did the speaker bring the discussion to a close?
    Well   1   2   3   4   5   Badly
    What was done?
    Was a final summary used?

23. *Timing*
    How well did the speaker keep within the time constraints?
    Completely   1   2   3   4   5   Badly

24. *Appropriate approach*
    Was this the most appropriate tactical approach for this subject
    or group?
    If not, which approach might have been more appropriate?

25. *Overall rating*
How would you rate the presentation of the session overall?
Excellent   1   2   3   4   5   Poor

26. *Any other comments*

Appendix Three

Activity Control

Checklist

1. Opening of session
2. Sincerity
3. Enthusiasm
4. Setting the scene
5. Introducing the topic
6. Visual aids
7. Visual aids relevancy
8. Visual aids quality
9. Visual aids use
10. Activity description
11. Activity stages description
12. Activity briefs
13. Observers
14. Observer briefs
15. Trainer interventions
16. Activity feedback
17. Activity feedback (2)
18. Summary
19. Appropriateness of activity
20. Appropriateness of type of activity
21. Any other comments

Trainer Assessment Guide

Activity control

1. *Opening of session*
   To what extent did the trainer obtain attention from the start?
   Great deal   1   2   3   4   5   Little
   How?

2. *Sincerity*
   How sincere and committed to the subject did the trainer appear
   to be?
   Very   1   2   3   4   5   Not at all
   How did this appear?

3. *Enthusiasm*
   How enthusiastic was the trainer's manner?
   Very   1   2   3   4   5   Not at all
   In what way?

4. *Setting the scene*
   To what extent did the trainer prepare the activity area(s) before
   the start of the discussion?
   Well   1   2   3   4   5   Not at all
   How?

5. *Introducing the topic*
   How well did the trainer introduce the activity?
   Clearly   1   2   3   4   5   In a confused manner
   What was the introduction?

6. *Visual aids*
   To what extent did the speaker use visual aids to introduce the
   activity?
   A great deal   1   2   3   4   5   None

7. *Visual aids relevancy*
   To what extent were the visual aids, if used, relevant to the
   situation?
   Very   1   2   3   4   5   Not at all
   Why?

8. *Visual aids quality*
   What was the quality of the visual aids used?
   Excellent   1   2   3   4   5   Poor
   In what way?

9. *Visual aids use*
   How effectively were the visual aids used?
   Very well   1   2   3   4   5   Badly
   What were the uses?

10. *Activity description*
    How clear was the trainer's description of the activity?
    Very clear   1   2   3   4   5   Not clear
    What was used?

11. *Activity stages description*
    How clear was the trainer's description of the stages of the
    activity?
    Very clear   1   2   3   4   5   Not clear
    How was this described?

12. *Activity briefs*
    How clear were the activity briefs issued to the participants?
    Very clear   1   2   3   4   5   Not clear
    In what way?

13. *Observers*
    How clear were the roles of the observers made?
    Very clear   1   2   3   4   5   Not clear
    Why?

14. *Observer briefs*
    How clear were the observers' briefs or observation forms?
    Very clear   1   2   3   4   5   Not clear
    How?

15. *Trainer interventions*
    To what extent did the trainer make appropriate interventions
    during the activity?
    Appropriately   1   2   3   4   5   Inappropriately
    What interventions were made?

16. *Activity review*
    How appropriate was the *method* of activity review?
    Very   1   2   3   4   5   Inappropriate
    Why?

17. *Activity review 2*
    How well did the trainer control the review?
    Very well   1   2   3   4   5   Badly
    How?

18. *Summary*
    How well did the trainer summarize the lessons relating to the
    activity?
    Very well 1 2 3 4 5 Badly
    What happened?

19. *Appropriateness of activity*
    How appropriate was the activity in this event?
    Appropriate 1 2 3 4 5 Inappropriate
    Why was this so?

20. *Appropriateness of type of activity*
    How appropriate was the type of activity used?
    Appropriate 1 2 3 4 5 Inappropriate
    For what reasons?

21. *Any other comments*

Appendix Four

Practical Demonstrations

Checklist

1. Introduction of subject
2. Description of object
3. Description of end result
4. Operation stages
5. Operation demonstration
6. Operating steps demonstration
7. Operating steps progression
8. Testing understanding
9. Questioning
10. Learner descriptions
11. Learner demonstrations
12. Appraisal of the learners
13. Learner control
14. Further practice
15. Overall performance
16. Relationship with co-trainer
17. Any other comments

Trainer Assessment Guide

Practical demonstrations

1. *Introduction of subject*
   How well were the objectives for the session presented?
   Very clearly   1   2   3   4   5   Unclearly
   How?

2. *Description of object*
   How well was the object described at the start of the sessions?
   Very well   1   2   3   4   5   Badly
   In what way?

3. *Descriptions of end result*
   How well was the purpose of the object or the end result of its operation described at the start?
   Very well   1   2   3   4   5   Badly
   Why?

4. *Operating stages*
   How clearly were the operating stages described?
   Very clearly   1   2   3   4   5   Unclearly
   In what way?

5. *Operation demonstration*
   How well was the operation of the object demonstrated?
   Very well   1   2   3   4   5   Badly
   What happened?

6. *Operating steps demonstration*
   How clearly were the progressive operating steps demonstrated?
   Very clearly   1   2   3   4   5   Unclearly

7. *Operating steps progression*
   How well were the learners led through the practical steps of the session?
   Very well   1   2   3   4   5   Badly
   What happened?

8. *Testing understanding*
   To what extent did the trainer clarify understanding by asking questions?
   Extensively   1   2   3   4   5   Rarely
   What was done?

9. *Questioning*
   How appropriate were the types of questions in testing understanding?
   Appropriate   1   2   3   4   5   Inappropriate

10. *Learner descriptions*
    To what extent did the trainer require the learners to describe the object and its operation?

Completely   1   2   3   4   5   Incompletely
What happened?

11. *Learner demonstrations*
    To what extent did the trainer require the learners to demon-
    strate the operation of the object?
    Completely   1   2   3   4   5   Incompletely
    How?

12. *Appraisal of the learners*
    How effective was the trainer's appraisal of the learner's practi-
    cal performance?
    Very effective   1   2   3   4   5   Ineffective

13. *Learner control*
    To what extent did the trainer recognize whether all the learners
    were with the trainer during the session?
    Completely   1   2   3   4   5   Not at all
    What happened?

14. *Further practice*
    What opportunities were given to the learners for further
    practice?
    Many   1   2   3   4   5   None
    In what way?

15. *Overall performance*
    How well did the trainer provide the demonstration?
    Very well   1   2   3   4   5   Badly

16. *Relationship with co-trainer (if relevant)*
    How well does the trainer relate to the co-trainer?
    To the appropriate extent   1   2   3   4   5   Not at all

17. *Any other comments*

Appendix Five

Lecture, Discussion Leading, and Activity Control Sessions

Checklist

Common aspects

1. Opening platform presence
2. Opening of session
3. Continuation of session
4. Session objectives
5. Eye contact (showing interest)
6. Sincerity
7. Enthusiasm
8. General manner
9. Voice
10. Timing
11. Pace
12. Appropriate approach
13. Creativity
14. Use of group
15. Bringing-in
16. Dealing with various members

Lecture section

17. Visual aids
18. Visual aids relevance

19. Visual aids quality
20. Visual aids use
21. Subject coverage
22. Use of session notes
23. Response to questions
24. Handouts—adequacy
25. Handouts 2—relevance
26. Pace

Discussion leading

27. Setting the scene
28. Introducing the topic
29. Discussion notes
30. Use of discussion notes
31. Use of questions
32. Types of questions
33. Response to questions
34. Listening
35. Interventions
36. Value of interventions
37. Closing the discussion

Activity control

38. Setting the scene
39. Introducing the topic
40. Activity description
41. Activity stages description
42. Activity briefs
43. Observers
44. Observer briefs
45. Trainer interventions
46. Activity feedback
47. Activity feedback (2)

48. Summary
49. Appropriateness of activity
50. Appropriateness of type of activity

Final common aspects

51. Satisfaction of objectives
52. Overall performance
    During lecture
    During discussion section
    During activity section
53. Any other comments

Lecture, Discussion Leading, and Activity Control Sessions

Common aspects

1. *Opening platform presence*
   To what extent did the trainer exhibit nervousness during the opening stages?
   None   1   2   3   4   5   A lot
   How?

   How did it disappear as the session continued?
   Quickly   1   2   3   4   5   Not at all

2. *Opening of session*
   To what extent did the speaker obtain attention from the start?
   A great deal   1   2   3   4   5   Little
   How?

3. *Continuation of the session*
   To what extent did the speaker maintain attention as the session progressed?
   All the time   1   2   3   4   5   Lost it
   How?

4. *Session objectives*
   How well were the objectives for the session introduced?
   Very well   1   2   3   4   5   Inadequately
   In what way?

5. *Eye contact (showing interest)*
   To what extent did the speaker maintain eye contact with the group?
   When speaking
   Most of time 1 2 3 4 5 Rarely
   In which way?

   When listening
   Most of time 1 2 3 4 5 Rarely
   In which way?

6. *Sincerity*
   How sincere and committed to the subject did the speaker appear to be?
   Very 1 2 3 4 5 Not at all
   How did this show?

7. *Enthusiasm*
   How enthusiastic was the speaker's manner?
   Very 1 2 3 4 5 Not at all
   How was this evidenced?

8. *General manner*
   To what extent did the speaker's manner relax you and encourage you to listen?
   A great deal 1 2 3 4 5 Little
   Which distractive mannerisms were present?

9. *Voice*
   How clear to the whole group was the speaker?
   Very clear 1 2 3 4 5 Unclear
   If unclear or tending toward unclear, in what way?

   How appropriate was the language used?
   Appropriate 1 2 3 4 5 Inappropriate

   If inappropriate or tending towards inappropriate, in what way?

10. *Timing*
    How well did the speaker keep within the time constraints?
    Completely 1 2 3 4 5 Badly
    What were the principal causes?

11. *Pace*
    How well did the trainer pace the complete session?
    Very well 1 2 3 4 5 Badly
    How?

12. *Appropriate approach*
Was this the most appropriate tactical approach for this subject or group?
If not, which approach might be more appropriate?

13. *Creativity*
To what extent was creativity of approach, methods, resources, and so on practiced as required?
Fully 1 2 3 4 5 Not at all
In what circumstances?

14. *Use of group*
To what extent did the leader bring in the quiet members?
A great deal 1 2 3 4 5 Not at all

15. *Bringing-in*
How did the leader bring in the quiet members?
With skill 1 2 3 4 5 Clumsily
How?

16. *Dealing with various members*
How well did the leader deal with difficult members?
Well 1 2 3 4 5 Badly
How?

Lecture section

17. *Visual aids*
To what extent did the speaker use visual aids to vary the presentation?
A great deal 1 2 3 4 5 None
In what way?

18. *Visual aids relevance*
How relevant to the training were the visual aids?
Relevant 1 2 3 4 5 Not relevant
Why?

19. *Visual aids quality*
What was the quality of the visual aids used?
Excellent 1 2 3 4 5 Poor
Why?

20. *Visual aids use*
How effectively were the visual aids used?
Very well 1 2 3 4 5 Badly
How?

21. *Subject coverage*
How well within the objectives was the subject covered?
Completely 1 2 3 4 5 Poorly
What was omitted or unclear?

22. *Use of session notes*
Was the use of session notes distracting?
Not at all 1 2 3 4 5 Very much
In what way?

23. *Response to questions*
How well did the speaker respond to questions from the group?
Very well 1 2 3 4 5 Badly
How?

24. *Handouts*
How adequate were the handouts?
Adequate 1 2 3 4 5 Inadequate
How?

25. *Handouts 2*
How relevant were the handouts?
Relevant 1 2 3 4 5 Not relevant
Why?

26. *Pace*
How well did the trainer pace the presentation?
Very well 1 2 3 4 5 Badly
How?

Discussion leading

27. *Setting the scene*
To what extent did the trainer prepare the discussion areas before the start of the discussion?
Well 1 2 3 4 5 Not at all
In what way?

28. *Introducing the topic*
How well did the trainer introduce the topic for discussion?
Clearly 1 2 3 4 5 In a confused manner
How?

29. *Discussion notes*
Did the trainer have a prepared discussion note sheet/shopping list?
Yes/no

30. *Use of discussion notes*
If the trainer had discussion notes, how well were they used?
Unobtrusively   1   2   3   4   5   Obtrusively
How?

31. *Use of questions*
How well did the leader use questions to the group?
Very well   1   2   3   4   5   Badly
In what way?

32. *Types of question*
Which types of question did the leader use more than others
(place in descending order of use as far as possible)

Open	Closed
Multiple	Hypothetical
Leading	Aggressive
Multiple choice	Reflective
Testing understanding	Others

33. *Response to questions*
How well did the speaker respond to questions from the group?
Very well   1   2   3   4   5   Badly
In what way?

34. *Listening*
To what extent did the leader appear to listen when the group
members were talking?
Fully   1   2   3   4   5   Not at all
What were the indications of this extent of listening?

35. *Interventions*
To what extent did the leader intervene in the discussion?
Rarely   1   2   3   4   5   Often

36. *Value of intervention*
When the leader intervened, were these interventions
Appropriate   1   2   3   4   5   Inappropriate
In what way?

37. *Closing the discussion*
How well did the speaker bring the discussion to a close?
Well   1   2   3   4   5   Badly
In what way?
Was a final summary used?

Activity

38. *Setting the scene*
    To what extent did the trainer prepare the activity area(s) before the start of the discussion?
    Well   1   2   3   4   5   Not at all
    How?

39. *Introducing the topic*
    How well did the trainer introduce the activity?
    Clearly   1   2   3   4   5   In a confused manner
    How?

40. *Activity description*
    How clear was the trainer's description of the activity?
    Very clear   1   2   3   4   5   Not clear
    In what way?

41. *Activity stages description*
    How clear was the trainer's description of the stages of the activity?
    Very clear   1   2   3   4   5   Not clear
    In what way?

42. *Activity briefs*
    How clear were the activity briefs issued to the participants?
    Very clear   1   2   3   4   5   Not clear
    How?

43. *Observers*
    How clear were the roles of the observers made?
    Very clear   1   2   3   4   5   Not clear
    In what way?

44. *Observer briefs*
    How clear were the observers' briefs or observation forms?
    Very clear   1   2   3   4   5   Not clear
    How?

45. *Trainer intervention*
    To what extent did the trainer make appropriate interventions during the activity?
    Appropriately   1   2   3   4   5   Inappropriately
    In what way?

46. *Activity review*
    How appropriate was the method of activity review?

Very   1   2   3   4   5   Inappropriate
In what way?

47. *Activity review 2*
How well did the trainer control the review?
Very well   1   2   3   4   5   Badly
In what way?

48. *Summary*
How well did the trainer summarize the lessons relating to the activity?
Very well   1   2   3   4   5   Badly
How?

49. *Appropriateness of activity?*
How appropriate was the activity in this event?
Appropriate   1   2   3   4   5   Inappropriate
Why?

50. *Appropriateness of type of activity*
How appropriate was the type of activity used?
Appropriate   1   2   3   4   5   Inappropriate
Why?

51. *Satisfaction of objectives*
To what extent were the session objectives satisfied?
Completely   1   2   3   4   5   Not at all
Why?

52. *Overall performance*
How well did the trainer perform during the lecture section?
Very well   1   2   3   4   5   Badly

How well did the trainer perform during the discussion section?
Very well   1   2   3   4   5   Badly

How well did the trainer perform during the activity section?
Very well   1   2   3   4   5   Badly

Any additional reasons other than those referred to in previous parts?

53. *Any other comments*

Assessment of Trainer by Trainees

Trainer Assessment

Course ....

Please complete the following questions by placing a tick or other mark against each question under the heading that most nearly represents your view.

It will help the trainer and his manager in the trainer's development if you would complete the questionnaire fully and honestly. There is no intention to use it in any way as a discipline document and it will support other assessments of the trainer's effectiveness.

	To a Large Extent	Partly	Hardly at All
1. To what extent did he create interest from the start?			
2. How much did he maintain this interest?			
3. To what extent did he declare the objectives of the course?			
4. To what extent did he just *tell* you?			
5. How much did he involve the group?			
6. How much did he use visual/audio aids?			
7. Were the aids of good quality?			
8. Were the aids relevant?			
9. How much variety was there in the course?			

	To a Large Extent	Partly	Hardly at All
10. How much use of summaries did he make?	_____	_____	_____
11. To what extent was the language used understandable?	_____	_____	_____
12. How much enthusiasm did he show?	_____	_____	_____
13. To what extent did he listen to the group?	_____	_____	_____
14. How much opportunity was the group given to pose questions?	_____	_____	_____
15. How much did his platform presence distract you?	_____	_____	_____
16. To what extent was he responsible for what you learned?	_____	_____	_____
17. Any other comments.	_____	_____	_____

Index